The Clinical
Documentation
Sourcebook

The Clinical Documentation Sourcebook

A Comprehensive Collection of
Mental Health Practice
FORMS, HANDOUTS, and RECORDS

Donald E. Wiger

John Wiley & Sons, Inc.
New York • Chichester • Weinheim • Brisbane • Singapore • Toronto

Copyright © 1997 by John Wiley & Sons, Inc.
Published by John Wiley & Sons, Inc.

Diagnostic criteria taken from DSM-IV reprinted with permission from
the Diagnostic and Statistical Manual of Mental Disorders, Fourth Edition.
Copyright 1994 American Psychiatric Association.

IBM is a registered trademark of International Business Machines Corporation.
WordPerfect is a registered trademark of Corel Corporation Limited.
Microsoft and Windows are registered trademarks of Microsoft Corporation.

Library of Congress Cataloging-in-Publication Data
Wiger, Donald E., 1953–
    The clinical documentation sourcebook : a comprehensive collection
of mental health practice forms, handouts, and records / by Donald
E. Wiger.
        p.   cm.
    Includes bibliographical references.
    ISBN 0-471-17934-5 (paper : alk. paper)
    1. Psychiatry—Medical records—Forms.   2. Mental health services—
Medical records—Forms.   I. Title.
    [DNLM: 1. Mental Health Services—standards.   2. Documentation—
methods.   3. Forms and Records Control—methods.   4. Medical
Records—standards.   WM 30 W654c 1997]
RC455.2.M38W54   1997
616.89′0068—dc21   96-39067
                                                        CIP

Printed in the United States of America
10 9 8 7 6 5 4 3 2 1

This book is dedicated to my two youngest daughters,
Cynthia, age five, and Victoria, age four,
who would not let me work on
the manuscript when they were awake.
To them I remain, "Daddy."

Contents

Introduction

Few mental health professionals have received graduate training in documentation procedures. Learning to write case notes, treatment plans, and other documentation is usually a trial-and-error process, often resulting in vague treatment plans, case notes, and therapy. Historically, case notes and treatment plans have been required in most mental health care settings, but few standardized procedures have been acknowledged. In many cases the mere existence of various forms and documents in clients' files was sufficient.

Historically, documentation procedures in medical fields other than mental health have been quite stringent, requiring that specific interventions be accurately charted. Without such documentation, physicians and nurses are understandably vulnerable to litigation. But, prior to the emergence of managed care, most mental health professions received little scrutiny by third-party payers in areas of accountability. Managed care changed the rules by raising the standards of documentation procedures in the mental health field.

In order for managed care companies to obtain contracts, they must attempt to provide the best services for the least money. Often, a few managed care companies cover a significant number of people in a given geographic area. To receive a sufficient number of referrals, mental health providers contract with these companies, but may become dissatisfied with demanding documentation rules and regulations.

Graduate training programs have concentrated on traditional therapeutic methods, teaching therapists to attend to clients, conceptualize cases, listen empathically, render interpretations, ease clients' emotional pain, provide direction, and slowly taper off the sessions to prevent relapse. Although such procedures and interventions are therapeutically necessary, third-party requirements rarely mention them because in themselves they do not necessarily document the efficacy and course of therapy. Instead, terms often not learned in graduate school such as "medical necessity," "functional impairment," and "discharge criteria" have become the criteria for continued services.

Procedural requirements and changes catalyzed by managed care for documentation of therapy have increased cognitive dissonance in mental health professionals. Dissonance has developed because therapists are being challenged by discrepancies between their established mental health procedures and seemingly conflicting new requirements that are often viewed as limiting the clinician's therapeutic freedom. The resulting cognitive dissonance leads to stress, discomfort, worry, and complaints. To say that managed care regulations and procedures have caused cognitive dissonance is an understatement like the observations that "Sigmund Freud had some sort of effect on psychology" or "Albert Einstein was smart."

It is possible to reduce cognitive dissonance by focusing on the benefits of documentation procedures. Effective documentation holds mental health professionals accountable for accurate diagnosis, concise treatment planning, case notes that follow the treatment plan, treatment reflecting the diagnosis, and documentation of the course of therapy.

Effective case notes can be written in a manner that would enable a new therapist to review a file and clearly determine specific impairments, the effectiveness of previous treatment strategies, client compliance, progress and setbacks.

Treatment does not necessarily have to change, but documentation procedures validating the effectiveness of treatment must be learned in order for mental health services to survive in the world of managed care. The ethical implications of being accountable (or not being accountable) for work deserves attention.

Managed care has brought the mental health profession up to par with other health care professionals in accountability procedures. In other areas of health care, the "black box" treatment approach—in which specific interventions are not documented—would be considered unethical, not reimbursable, and open to litigation. Without clear documentation procedures there is little or no accountability, leaving professionals open to allegations of fraud due to lack of specific evidence that necessary services are being provided.

For example, one major managed care company (Blue Cross/Blue Shield) has established the following (selected) requirements and criteria for mental health services to be eligible for benefits:

1. "Services must be medically and/or therapeutically necessary." Medical necessity is determined by "the presence of significant impairment or dysfunction in the performance of activities and/or responsibilities of daily living as a result of a mental disorder." Note that the emphasis is on the impairment, not simply the diagnosis. Although most third-party payers require an Axis I diagnosis, it is the resulting impairment that is the focus of interventions.

2. "Therapeutic necessity is defined as services consistent with the diagnosis and impairment which are non-experimental in nature and can be reliably predicted to positively affect the patient's condition." Therapeutic interventions must have a positive track record for the particular diagnosis and impairments. Charting procedures that do not clearly and consistently reflect such interventions do not document therapeutic necessity.

3. "The intensity of treatment must be consistent with the acuity and severity of the patient's current level of impairment and/or dysfunction." Without regular documentation of current functioning (session by session) and a rationale for the intensity of treatment, no evidence exists.

4. "There must be documentation of reasonable progress consistent with the intensity of treatment and the severity of the disorder." Case notes must validate the effectiveness of the current therapeutic interventions and justify the frequency of sessions.

5. ". . . documented, specific evidence of a diagnosable mental disorder (based on current DSM). The diagnosis must be validated by *Diagnostic and Statistical Manual of Mental Disorders* (DSM) criteria. A diagnosis is more than an opinion: Specific symptoms must be documented according to current DSM-IV criteria.

6. "The treatment plan includes specific, objective, behavioral goals for discharge." Both the client and the therapist have agreed on discharge criteria, stated in behavioral measures.

7. Justification to continue treatment includes "persistence of significant symptoms and impairment or dysfunction resultant from mental illness which required continued treatment including impaired social, familial or occupational functioning or evidence of symptoms which reflects potential dangers to self, others and/or property." Case notes must regularly document the persistence of impairment. Without this documentation, there is no evidence and therefore the impairment and diagnosis no longer exist (as far as documentation is concerned). It is possible that a significant impairment may exist, but if it is not appropriately documented, payment for services could be discontinued.

8. "Insufficient behavioral and/or dysfunctional evidence is present to support the current diagnosis." Not only must impairments be documented, but the DSM Axis I diagnosis must be documented with evidence throughout the course of therapy. If the diagnosis is not supported throughout the case notes, there is no evidence, and therefore third-party payment may be halted.

9. "Lack of therapeutic appropriateness and/or lack of therapeutic progress." Evidence of therapeutic gains and setbacks are required documentation procedures.

10. Noncovered services include services without a "definite treatment plan," services without corresponding documentation, medically unnecessary services, services without a diagnosable mental disorder, and several other uncovered services.

The above summary of third-party documentation procedures indicates specific requirements that are designed to document the efficacy of therapy in such areas as validation of diagnosis, functional impairments, symptoms, treatment, client cooperation, and providing behavioral evidence of gains and setbacks in treatment. Benefits of learning these procedures range from increased prior authorization approval for additional sessions, to clearer focus in therapy, to audit survival.

Sample forms and related examples of several documentation procedures from the initial client contact to the discharge summary are included. Blank forms are provided along with several of the forms filled out. Unless a form is self-explanatory, explanations are provided on its use. Special emphasis is placed on treatment plans and case notes.

Organization

This book is organized into six chapters of forms and procedures in the areas of intake and termination, assessment for counseling, evaluations, treatment plans, case notes, and relationship counseling.

Brief explanations of each form are followed by examples of forms filled out and then blank forms, which may be copied.

Judy Doe

An ongoing case example of a client named Judy Doe will be used in many of the documentation procedures and forms throughout the book.

The Clinical
Documentation
Sourcebook

Chapter 1

Intake and Termination Forms and Procedures

The mental health clinic's intake information forms elicit demographic and payment information about the client. They also communicate business, legal, and ethical issues and responsibilities. Although initial intake forms do not provide specific clinical information, they do provide an understanding of the responsibilities of both the client and the clinic. In each case, these forms are taken care of prior to the first counseling session. All insurance and financial agreements are contracted with the client before services begin. The clinic's financial policies must be clearly spelled out. In addition, the client should be made aware of, and agree to, the limits of confidentiality in a counseling session.

Common client questions are: "What if my insurance company does not pay?," "How confidential is the session?," "Do parents have the right to their children's records?," "What happens if payment is not received?," "What happens if suicide is mentioned?," and "What is the price of therapy?" These and other questions are not only answered, but also documented and signed. Any of these issues, if not covered, could lead to misunderstandings, subsequent premature termination of treatment, ethics charges, or a lawsuit. Intake forms provide clear communication between the client and clinic, with the aim of eliminating misunderstandings detrimental to the therapeutic process and clinic survival.

Initial Client Information Form

The initial intake information form (see page 1.5) is filled out at the time of the referral or initial client contact with the mental health care provider. Information solicited from the client includes basic demographics, plus insurance identification information. For insurance reasons, information requested from the client should minimally include:

- Policyholder information: name, date of birth, social security number, policy number.

- Similar information from family members receiving services.

- Name of employer.

- Name and telephone number of each third-party payer.

If the mental health care provider processes insurance information, it is crucial to verify benefits from the insurance company. Specific questions should be asked of the third party, minimally including the following:

- Persons covered by the policy.

- Deductible amount and amount currently satisfied.

- Co-payment amounts.

- Limits of policy.

- Covered/noncovered services (e.g., individual, family, relationship).

- Prior authorizations needed.

- Coverage and policies for testing.

- Supervision required for various providers.

- Type(s) of provider(s) covered for services (e.g., psychologist, social worker counselor).

- Policy anniversary date.

When the above information is unclear or unknown, there is room for misunderstanding between the mental health care provider and the client. Clients usually believe that all services performed in therapy are covered by their insurance. But mental health benefits from several sources are decreasing, and only specific, limited services are now covered. For example, just a few years ago several third-party payers paid for testing; today testing is seldom considered a standard procedure and often needs prior approval.

Another trend is that most managed-care companies approve only a few sessions at a time, while in the past few restrictions were made.

Initial insurance information provided by third-party payers is not a guarantee of benefits. Each mental health care provider should have a clear financial policy and payment contract (possibly on the same form) to explain conditions of payment in the event that the third-party payer denies payment.

Initial Client Information

Name __Judy Doe__ Intake Date _3-8-97_ Time _9:00 a.m._

Address __123 Main St.__ Therapist Requested Y __ N _X_

Pleasantville, NJ 99999 Therapist __DLB__ Office __SP__

Source of Referral __YP__ Type(s) of Service _Individual_

Home Phone __555-5555__ Work Phone __555-5544__ Birth Date _7-6-48_

[X] Primary Insurance Company __United Cross Healthcare__

Address __5678 9th St.__ __Pleasantville__ __NJ__ __99998__
  Number   City   State   Zip

Phone Number __555-3344__ Persons Covered __All family members__

Contact Person __Sheryl Sperry__ M&F Covered __No__

Policy Holder __Judy Doe__ Policy Number __1234567__

Employer/Group _Pleasantville School Dis. 22_ SS Number __999-99-9999__

PROVISIONS Client pays $__100__ Deductible Amount Amount Satisfied $__50__

Insurance pays __80__ % for visits __1__ - __10__ and __75__ % for visits __11__ - __30__

Type(s) of providers covered _Indiv, Family, Group, Assessment_ Supervision _None if licensed_

Prior Authorization Needed _After session 5 need PA. All testing_

Effective Date _Jan. 1, 1997_ Policy Anniversary _Dec. 31, 1997_

Coverage for Testing _Annual limit: $400_ Annual Limit _(total) $2000.00_

Other 3rd Party Coverage _____

Address __None__
  Number   City   State   Zip

Phone Number _____ Persons Covered _____

Contact Person _____ M&F Covered _____

Policy Holder _____ Policy Number _____

Other Provisions _____

[X] Personal Payment Amount $_____ Terms _as incurred_

Payment Method (Insurance and Cash clients; deductibles, co-payments, etc.)
___Check ___Cash _X_ Charge Card (type) _Discover_ Number _1234-5678-9012-3456_

Cardholder's Name _Judy Doe_ Expires _8-99_

Completed	_X_ Entered System	Date _3-5-97_
Procedures	_X_ Confirmed Insurance	Date _3-5-97_
	_X_ Confirmed with Client	Date _3-5-97_

Initial Client Information

Name_____ Intake Date _____ Time _____

Address _____ Therapist Requested   Y__   N__

_____ Therapist _____ Office _____

Source of Referral _____ Type(s) of Service _____

Home Phone_____ Work Phone _____ Birth Date_____

☐ Primary Insurance Company _____

Address _____
         Number   City   State   Zip

Phone Number _____ Persons Covered _____

Contact Person _____ M&F Covered _____

Policy Holder _____ Policy Number _____

Employer/Group_____ SS Number _____

PROVISIONS   Client pays $_____ Deductible Amount   Amount Satisfied $_____

Insurance pays _____% for visits _____-_____ and _____% for visits _____-_____

Type(s) of providers covered _____ Supervision _____

Prior Authorization Needed _____

Effective Date _____ Policy Anniversary_____

Coverage for Testing _____ Annual Limit _____

Other 3rd Party Coverage _____

Address _____
         Number   City   State   Zip

Phone Number _____ Persons Covered _____

Contact Person _____ M&F Covered _____

Policy Holder _____ Policy Number _____

Other Provisions _____

_____

☐ Personal Payment Amount $_____ Terms _____

Payment Method (Insurance and Cash clients; deductibles, co-payments, etc.)
___Check   ___Cash   ___Charge Card (type) _____ Number _____

Cardholder's Name_____ Expires _____

Completed	___ Entered System	Date _____
Procedures	___ Confirmed Insurance	Date _____
	___ Confirmed with Client	Date _____

Financial Policy Statement

Clinical skills are necessary, but not the sole component in the overall scope of mental health services. A concise, written financial policy is crucial to the successful operation of any practice. Clear financial policies and procedures eliminate much potential discord (and premature termination of services) between the client and the therapist and clinic. Clinics that thrive financially and are self-sufficient have few accounts receivable at any time. An adequate financial policy statement addresses the following:

- The client is ultimately responsible for payment to the clinic. The clinic can not guarantee insurance benefits. (*Note:* Some managed-care contracts forbid client payment to the clinic for noncovered services without permission.)

- Clinics that bill insurance companies should convey to clients the fact that billing third-party payers is simply a service—not a responsibility—of the clinic.

- There are time limits in waiting for insurance payments, after which the client must pay the clinic. Some clinics collect the entire amount initially from the client and reimburse the client when insurance money is received.

- The clinic's policy regarding payment for treatment of minors should be noted.

- The policy regarding payment for charges not covered by third-party payers should be addressed.

- The financial policy form should be signed by the person(s) responsible for payment.

- Assignment of benefit policies should be addressed.

- The financial policy statement should specify when payments are due and policies for nonpayment.

- Methods of payment should be listed.

Request clients to read and sign the financial policy statement prior to the first session (see page 1.8). Some mental health providers ask clients to come to the first session 15 to 20 minutes early to review the initial policies and procedures. Take care of all financial understandings with the client before the first session begins; otherwise, valuable session time might be taken up reviewing financial issues.

Financial Policy

The staff at *(Name of Clinic or Therapist)* (hereafter referred to as the clinic) are committed to providing caring and professional mental health care to all of our clients. As part of the delivery of mental health services we have established a financial policy which provides payment policies and options to all consumers. The financial policy of the clinic is designed to clarify the payment policies as determined by the management of the clinic.

The Person Responsible for Payment of Account is required to sign the form, *Payment Contract for Services*, which explains the fees and collection policies of the clinic. Your insurance policy, if any, is a contract between you and the insurance company; we are not part of the contract with you and your insurance company.

As a service to you, the clinic will bill insurance companies and other third-party payers, but can not guarantee such benefits or the amounts covered, and is not responsible for the collection of such payments. In some cases insurance companies or other third-party payers may consider certain services as not reasonable or necessary or may determine that services are not covered. In such cases the Person Responsible for Payment of Account is responsible for payment of these services. We charge our clients the usual and customary rates for the area. Clients are responsible for payments regardless of any insurance company's arbitrary determination of usual and customary rates.

The Person Responsible for Payment (as noted in the Payment Contract for Services) will be financially responsible for payment of such services. The Person Responsible for Payment of Account is financially responsible for paying funds not payed by insurance companies or third-party payers after 60 days. Payments not received after 120 days are subject to collections. A 1% per month interest rate is charged for accounts over 60 days.

Insurance deductibles and co-payments are due at the time of service. Although it is possible that mental health coverage deductible amounts may have been met elsewhere (e.g., if there were previous visits to another mental health provider since January of the current year that were prior to the first session at the clinic), this amount will be collected by the clinic until the deductible payment is verified to the clinic by the insurance company or third-party provider.

All insurance benefits will be assigned to this clinic (by insurance company or third-party provider) unless the Person Responsible for Payment of Account pays the entire balance each session.

Clients are responsible for payments at the time of services. The adult accompanying a minor (or guardian of the minor) is responsible for payments for the child at the time of service. Unaccompanied minors will be denied nonemergency service unless charges have been preauthorized to an approved credit plan, charge card, or payment at the time of service.

Missed appointments or cancellations less than 24 hours prior to the appointment are charged a rate noted in the Payment Contract for Services.

Payments methods include check, cash, or the following charge cards: *Visa, MasterCard, Discover* . Clients using charge cards may either use their card at each session or sign a document allowing the clinic to automatically submit charges to the charge card after each session.

Questions regarding the financial policies can be answered by the Office Manager.

I (we) have read, understand, and agree with the provisions of the Financial Policy.

_____*Judy Doe*_____   _____*3-8-97*_____
Signature of Person Responsible for Payment of Account   Date

_____   _____
Signature of Co-responsible Party   Date

Financial Policy

The staff at (_____) (hereafter referred to as the clinic) are committed to providing caring and professional mental health care to all of our clients. As part of the delivery of mental health services we have established a financial policy which provides payment policies and options to all consumers. The financial policy of the clinic is designed to clarify the payment policies as determined by the management of the clinic.

The Person Responsible for Payment of Account is required to sign the form, *Payment Contract for Services*, which explains the fees and collection policies of the clinic. Your insurance policy, if any, is a contract between you and the insurance company; we are not part of the contract with you and your insurance company.

As a service to you, the clinic will bill insurance companies and other third-party payers, but can not guarantee such benefits or the amounts covered, and is not responsible for the collection of such payments. In some cases insurance companies or other third-party payers may consider certain services as not reasonable or necessary or may determine that services are not covered. In such cases the Person Responsible for Payment of Account is responsible for payment of these services. We charge our clients the usual and customary rates for the area. Clients are responsible for payments regardless of any insurance company's arbitrary determination of usual and customary rates.

The Person Responsible for Payment (as noted in the Payment Contract for Services) will be financially responsible for payment of such services. The Person Responsible for Payment of Account is financially responsible for paying funds not payed by insurance companies or third-party payers after 60 days. Payments not received after 120 days are subject to collections. A 1% per month interest rate is charged for accounts over 60 days.

Insurance deductibles and co-payments are due at the time of service. Although it is possible that mental health coverage deductible amounts may have been met elsewhere (e.g., if there were previous visits to another mental health provider since January of the current year that were prior to the first session at the clinic), this amount will be collected by the clinic until the deductible payment is verified to the clinic by the insurance company or third-party provider.

All insurance benefits will be assigned to this clinic (by insurance company or third-party provider) unless the Person Responsible for Payment of Account pays the entire balance each session.

Clients are responsible for payments at the time of services. The adult accompanying a minor (or guardian of the minor) is responsible for payments for the child at the time of service. Unaccompanied minors will be denied nonemergency service unless charges have been preauthorized to an approved credit plan, charge card, or payment at the time of service.

Missed appointments or cancellations less than 24 hours prior to the appointment are charged a rate noted in the Payment Contract for Services.

Payments methods include check, cash, or the following charge cards: _____.
Clients using charge cards may either use their card at each session or sign a document allowing the clinic to automatically submit charges to the charge card after each session.

Questions regarding the financial policies can be answered by the Office Manager.

I (we) have read, understand, and agree with the provisions of the Financial Policy.

_____   _____
Signature of Person Responsible for Payment of Account   Date

_____   _____
Signature of Co-responsible Party   Date

Payment Contract for Services

Along with the financial policy statement, the payment contract is vital for the clinic's financial survival. Without a payment contract, clients are not clearly obligated to pay for mental health services. The following payment contract meets federal criteria for a truth in lending disclosure statement for professional services and provides a release of information to bill third parties (see page 1.11).

The contract lists professional fees that will be charged. (A clinical hour should be defined by the number of minutes it covers rather than stating "per hour.") Interest rates on late payments must be disclosed. Other services provided by the mental health care provider must also be listed, and costs should be disclosed. Fees for services such as testing should be listed, either by the test or at an hourly rate for testing and interpretation time. The contract should cover specific clinic policies regarding missed appointments, outside consultations, and other potential fees related to the mental health care provider.

The mental health care provider may choose to include or omit estimated insurance benefits in the payment contract. Since the mental health clinic is not directly affiliated with the third-party payer and their changing policies, it is important to clearly state that payment is due regardless of decisions made by the third-party payer and that the client is financially responsible to the clinic for any amounts not paid by the third-party payer within a certain time frame.

Payment Contract for Services

Name(s): _Judy Doe_

Address: _123 Main St._   _Pleasantville_   _NJ_   _99998_

        Street   City   State   Zip

Bill to: Person(s) Responsible for Payment of Account _Same_

Address: _____

Federal Truth in Lending Disclosure Statement for Professional Services

Part One   **Fees for Professional Services**

I (we) agree to pay (_name of clinic or mental health provider_), hereafter referred to as the clinic, a rate of $ _100.00_ per clinical unit (defined as 45–50 minutes for assessment, testing, and individual, family, and relationship counseling). A fee of $ _25.00_ is charged for group counseling. The fee for testing includes scoring and report-writing time. A fee of $ _25.00_ is charged for missed appointments or cancellations with less than 24 hours' notice.

Part Two   **Clients with Insurance (Deductible and Co-payment Agreement)**

This clinic has been informed by either you or your insurance company that your policy contains (but is not limited to) the following provisions for mental health services:

Estimated Insurance Benefits

1) $ _100.00_   Deductible Amount (Paid by Insured Party)
2) Co-payment _20_ %   ($ _20_ /clinical unit) for first _10_ visits.
3) Co-payment _25_ %   ($ _25_ /clinical unit) up to _30_ visits.
4) The policy limit is _$2000.00_ per year: _X_ annual   ___ calendar

We suggest you confirm these provisions with the insurance company. The Person Responsible for Payment shall make payment for services which are not paid by your insurance policy, all co-payments, and deductibles. We will also attempt to verify these amounts with the insurance company.

Your insurance company may not pay for services that they consider to be nonefficacious, not medically or therapeutically necessary, or ineligible (not covered by your policy, or the policy has expired or is not in effect for you or other people receiving services). If the insurance company does not pay the estimated amount, you are responsible for the balance. The amounts charged for professional services are explained in Part One above.

Part Three   **All Clients**

Payments, co-payments, and deductible amounts are due at the time of service. There is a 1% per month (12% Annual Percentage Rate) interest charge on all accounts that are not paid within 60 days of the billing date.

I HEREBY CERTIFY that I have read and agree to the conditions and have received a copy of the Federal Truth in Lending Disclosure Statement for Professional Services.

Judy Doe / _____   _3-8-97_

Signature(s) of Person(s) Responsible for Payment   Date

Release of Information Authorization to Third Party

I (we) authorize _Name of Clinic or Therapist_ to disclose case records (diagnosis, case notes, psychological reports, testing results, or other requested material) to the above listed third-party payer or insurance company for the purpose of receiving payment reimbursement directly to _Name of Clinic or Therapist_.

I (we) understand that access to this information will be limited to determining insurance benefits, and will be accessible only to persons whose employment is to determine payments and/or insurance benefits. I (we) understand that I (we) may revoke this consent at any time by providing written notice, and after one year this consent expires. I (we) have been informed what information will be given, its purpose, and who will receive it. I (we) certify that I (we) have read and agree to the conditions and have received a copy of this form.

Judy Doe / _____   _3-8-97_

Signature(s) of Person(s) Responsible for Payment   Date

_____ / _____   _____

Signature(s) of Person(s) Receiving Services   Date

_____ / _____   _____

Signature(s) of Person(s) or Guardian(s)   Date

Payment Contract for Services

Name(s):_____

Address: _____
          Street   City   State   Zip

Bill to: Person(s) Responsible for Payment of Account _____

Address: _____

Federal Truth in Lending Disclosure Statement for Professional Services

Part One   **Fees for Professional Services**

I (we) agree to pay _____, hereafter referred to as the clinic, a rate of $_____
per clinical unit (defined as 45–50 minutes for assessment, testing, and individual, family, and relationship counseling).
A fee of $_____ is charged for group counseling. The fee for testing includes scoring and report-writing time.
A fee of $_____ is charged for missed appointments or cancellations with less than 24 hours' notice.

Part Two   **Clients with Insurance (Deductible and Co-payment Agreement)**

This clinic has been informed by either you or your insurance company that your policy contains (but is not limited to) the following provisions for mental health services:

Estimated Insurance Benefits

1) $_____ Deductible Amount (Paid by Insured Party)
2) Co-payment _____%   ($_____/clinical unit) for first_____ visits.
3) Co-payment_____%   ($_____/clinical unit) up to_____ visits.
4) The policy limit is _____per year: ___ annual   ___ calendar

We suggest you confirm these provisions with the insurance company. The Person Responsible for Payment shall make payment for services which are not paid by your insurance policy, all co-payments, and deductibles. We will also attempt to verify these amounts with the insurance company.

Your insurance company may not pay for services that they consider to be nonefficacious, not medically or therapeutically necessary, or ineligible (not covered by your policy, or the policy has expired or is not in effect for you or other people receiving services). If the insurance company does not pay the estimated amount, you are responsible for the balance. The amounts charged for professional services are explained in Part One above.

Part Three   **All Clients**

Payments, co-payments, and deductible amounts are due at the time of service. There is a 1% per month (12% Annual Percentage Rate) interest charge on all accounts that are not paid within 60 days of the billing date.

I HEREBY CERTIFY that I have read and agree to the conditions and have received a copy of the Federal Truth in Lending Disclosure Statement for Professional Services.

_____ / _____ _____
Signature(s) of Person(s) Responsible for Payment   Date

Release of Information Authorization to Third Party

I (we) authorize _____ to disclose case records (diagnosis, case notes, psychological reports, testing results, or other requested material) to the above listed third-party payer or insurance company for the purpose of receiving payment reimbursement directly to _____.

I (we) understand that access to this information will be limited to determining insurance benefits, and will be accessible only to persons whose employment is to determine payments and/or insurance benefits. I (we) understand that I (we) may revoke this consent at any time by providing written notice, and after one year this consent expires. I (we) have been informed what information will be given, its purpose, and who will receive it. I (we) certify that I (we) have read and agree to the conditions and have received a copy of this form.

_____ / _____ _____
Signature(s) of Person(s) Responsible for Payment   Date

_____ / _____ _____
Signature(s) of Person(s) Receiving Services   Date

_____ / _____ _____
Signature(s) of Person(s) or Guardian(s)   Date

Limits of Confidentiality Form

Accountability in the intake session goes far beyond providing an accurate diagnosis. Legal and ethical considerations must be addressed prior to eliciting personal intake information. As "informed consumers" of mental health services, clients are entitled to know how confidential their records are. Few people are aware of the potential risks of having a recorded Axis I diagnosis and how such a record might adversely affect the client.

While several books have been written regarding the ethics of informed consent, there are additional areas of informed consent usually not addressed in the intake process that could lead to litigation. Therapists should have a written document addressing the limits of confidentiality that is to be signed by the client (see page 1.15). Thirteen areas of confidentiality are noted below. The first seven are commonly known, while the remaining items are seldom considered.

1. *Duty to warn and protect.* When a client discloses intentions or a plan to harm another person, health care professionals are required to warn the intended victim and report this information to legal authorities. In cases in which the client discloses or implies a plan for suicide, health care professionals are required to notify legal authorities and make reasonable attempts to warn the family of the client.

2. *Abuse of children and vulnerable adults.* If a client states or suggests that he or she is abusing or has recently abused a child or vulnerable adult, or a child or vulnerable adult is in danger of abuse, health care professionals are required to report this information to the appropriate social service and/or legal authorities.

3. *Prenatal exposure to controlled substances.* Health care professionals are required to report admitted prenatal exposure to controlled substances that are potentially harmful. State laws may vary.

4. *In the event of a client's death.* In the event of a client's death, the spouse or parents of a deceased client have a right to gain access to their child's or spouse's records.

5. *Professional misconduct.* Professional misconduct by a health care professional must be reported by other health care professionals. If a professional or legal disciplinary meeting is held regarding

the health care professional's actions, related records may be released in order to substantiate disciplinary concerns.

6. *Court orders.* Health care professionals are required to release records of clients when a court order has been issued.

7. *Minors/guardianship.* Parents or legal guardians of nonemancipated minor clients have the right to gain access to the client's records.

8. *Collection agencies.* Although the use of collection agencies is not considered unethical, there may be ethical concerns if a client is not informed that the clinic uses collection agencies when fees are not paid in a timely manner. If use of a collection agency causes a client's credit report to list the name of the counseling agency, it is not uncommon for the client to threaten a lawsuit against a therapist claiming that confidentiality has been violated.

    A clear financial policy signed by the client prior to receiving services is crucial in the operation of a clinic. Clear financial policies and procedures eliminate much potential discord (and premature termination of services) between the client and the therapist and clinic. Clinics which thrive financially and are self-sufficient have few accounts receivable.

9. *Third-party payers.* Many clients using insurance to pay for services are not aware of potential drawbacks. They may not realize which of their mental health records may be available to third-party payers. Insurance companies may require and be entitled to information such as dates of service, diagnosis, treatment plans, descriptions of impairment, progress of therapy, case notes and summaries. The documented existence of an Axis I diagnosis could have adverse future effects on such areas as insurance benefits.

10. *Professional consultations.* Clients should be informed if their cases are discussed in staff meetings or professional consultations. Assure them that no identifying information will be disclosed.

11. *Typing/dictation services.* Confidentiality might be violated when anyone other than the therapist types psychological reports. In many cases office staff have access to records. There have been several cases in which office personnel have reviewed files of relatives, neighbors, and other acquaintances. This is difficult to prevent, so inform clients that clerical personnel might have access to records and are held accountable for confidentiality. Records should be available within a clinic only on a "need to know" basis.

12. *Couples, family, and relationship counseling.* Separate files should be kept for each person involved in any conjoint or family counseling. If more than one person's records are kept in one file, it is possible that a serious breach of confidentiality could take place. For example, when couples enter counseling for marital issues, there is a potential for divorce and a child custody battle. If one of the partners requests "their file" and receives confidential material about the spouse, confidentiality has been violated. A clear policy indicating the agency's procedures in such situations is needed.

13. *Telephone calls, answering machines, and voice mail.* In the event that the agency or mental health professional must telephone the client for purposes such as appointment cancellations, reminders, or to give/receive information, efforts must be made to preserve confidentiality. The therapist should ask the client to list where the agency may phone the client and what identifying information can be used.

Limits of Confidentiality

The contents of a counseling, intake, or assessment session are considered to be confidential. Both verbal information and written records about a client can not be shared with another party without the written consent of the client or the client's legal guardian. It is the policy of this clinic not to release any information about a client without a signed release of information. Noted exceptions are as follows:

Duty to Warn and Protect

When a client discloses intentions or a plan to harm another person, the health care professional is required to warn the intended victim and report this information to legal authorities. In cases in which the client discloses or implies a plan for suicide, the health care professional is required to notify legal authorities and make reasonable attempts to notify the family of the client.

Abuse of Children and Vulnerable Adults

If a client states or suggests that he or she is abusing a child (or vulnerable adult) or has recently abused a child (or vulnerable adult), or a child (or vulnerable adult) is in danger of abuse, the health care professional is required to report this information to the appropriate social service and/or legal authorities.

Prenatal Exposure to Controlled Substances

Health care professionals are required to report admitted prenatal exposure to controlled substances that are potentially harmful.

In the Event of a Client's Death

In the event of a client's death, the spouse or parents of a deceased client have a right to access their child's or spouse's records.

Professional Misconduct

Professional misconduct by a health care professional must be reported by other health care professionals. In cases in which a professional or legal disciplinary meeting is being held regarding the health care professional's actions, related records may be released in order to substantiate disciplinary concerns.

Court Orders

Health care professionals are required to release records of clients when a court order has been placed.

Minors/Guardianship

Parents or legal guardians of nonemancipated minor clients have the right to access the clients' records.

Other Provisions

When fees for services are not paid in a timely manner, collection agencies may be utilized in collecting unpaid debts. The specific content of the services (e.g., diagnosis, treatment plan, case notes, testing) is not disclosed. If a debt remains unpaid it may be reported to credit agencies, and the client's credit report may state the amount owed, time frame, and the name of the clinic.

Insurance companies and other third-party payers are given information that they request regarding services to clients. Information which may be requested includes type of services, dates/times of services, diagnosis, treatment plan, description of impairment, progress of therapy, case notes, and summaries.

Information about clients may be disclosed in consultations with other professionals in order to provide the best possible treatment. In such cases the name of the client, or any identifying information, is not disclosed. Clinical information about the client is discussed.

In some cases notes and reports are dictated/typed within the clinic or by outside sources specializing (and held accountable) for such procedures.

When couples, groups, or families are receiving services, separate files are kept for individuals for information disclosed that is of a confidential nature. This information includes (a) testing results, (b) information given to the mental health professional not in the presence of the other person(s) utilizing services, (c) information received from other sources about the client, (d) diagnosis, (e) treatment plan, (f) individual reports/summaries, and (h) information that has been requested to be separate. The material disclosed in conjoint family or couples sessions, in which each party discloses such information in each other's presence, is kept in each file in the form of case notes.

In the event in which the clinic or mental health professional must telephone the client for purposes such as appointment cancellations or reminders, or to give/receive other information, efforts are made to preserve confidentiality. Please list where we may reach you by phone and how you would like us to identify ourselves. For example, you might request that when we phone you at home or work, we do not say the name of the clinic or the nature of the call, but rather the mental health professional's first name only.

If this information is not provided to us (below), we will adhere to the following procedure when making phone calls: First we will ask to speak to the client (or guardian) without identifying the name of the clinic. If the person answering the phone asks for more identifying information we will say that it is a personal call. We will not identify the clinic (to protect confidentiality). If we reach an answering machine or voice mail we will follow the same guidelines.

PLEASE CHECK PLACES IN WHICH YOU MAY BE REACHED BY PHONE. Include phone numbers and how you would like us to identify ourselves when phoning you.

X HOME	_555-5555_	_1st name of therapist_	___ Yes	_X_ No
	Phone number	How should we identify ourselves?	May we say the clinic name?	
X WORK	_555-5544_	_1st name of therapist_	___ Yes	_X_ No
	Phone number	How should we identify ourselves?	May we say the clinic name?	
___ OTHER			___ Yes	___ No
	Phone number	How should we identify ourselves?	May we say the clinic name?	

I agree to the above limits of confidentiality and understand their meanings and ramifications.

_____Judy Doe_____	_____Judy Doe_____	_3-8-97_
Client's Name (please print)	Client's (or Guardian's) Signature	Date

Limits of Confidentiality

The contents of a counseling, intake, or assessment session are considered to be confidential. Both verbal information and written records about a client can not be shared with another party without the written consent of the client or the client's legal guardian. It is the policy of this clinic not to release any information about a client without a signed release of information. Noted exceptions are as follows:

Duty to Warn and Protect

When a client discloses intentions or a plan to harm another person, the health care professional is required to warn the intended victim and report this information to legal authorities. In cases in which the client discloses or implies a plan for suicide, the health care professional is required to notify legal authorities and make reasonable attempts to notify the family of the client.

Abuse of Children and Vulnerable Adults

If a client states or suggests that he or she is abusing a child (or vulnerable adult) or has recently abused a child (or vulnerable adult), or a child (or vulnerable adult) is in danger of abuse, the health care professional is required to report this information to the appropriate social service and/or legal authorities.

Prenatal Exposure to Controlled Substances

Health care professionals are required to report admitted prenatal exposure to controlled substances that are potentially harmful.

In the Event of a Client's Death

In the event of a client's death, the spouse or parents of a deceased client have a right to access their child's or spouse's records.

Professional Misconduct

Professional misconduct by a health care professional must be reported by other health care professionals. In cases in which a professional or legal disciplinary meeting is being held regarding the health care professional's actions, related records may be released in order to substantiate disciplinary concerns.

Court Orders

Health care professionals are required to release records of clients when a court order has been placed.

Minors/Guardianship

Parents or legal guardians of nonemancipated minor clients have the right to access the clients' records.

Other Provisions

When fees for services are not paid in a timely manner, collection agencies may be utilized in collecting unpaid debts. The specific content of the services (e.g., diagnosis, treatment plan, case notes, testing) is not disclosed. If a debt remains unpaid it may be reported to credit agencies, and the client's credit report may state the amount owed, time frame, and the name of the clinic.

Insurance companies and other third-party payers are given information that they request regarding services to clients. Information which may be requested includes type of services, dates/times of services, diagnosis, treatment plan, description of impairment, progress of therapy, case notes, and summaries.

Information about clients may be disclosed in consultations with other professionals in order to provide the best possible treatment. In such cases the name of the client, or any identifying information, is not disclosed. Clinical information about the client is discussed.

In some cases notes and reports are dictated/typed within the clinic or by outside sources specializing (and held accountable) for such procedures.

When couples, groups, or families are receiving services, separate files are kept for individuals for information disclosed that is of a confidential nature. This information includes (a) testing results, (b) information given to the mental health professional not in the presence of the other person(s) utilizing services, (c) information received from other sources about the client, (d) diagnosis, (e) treatment plan, (f) individual reports/summaries, and (h) information that has been requested to be separate. The material disclosed in conjoint family or couples sessions, in which each party discloses such information in each other's presence, is kept in each file in the form of case notes.

In the event in which the clinic or mental health professional must telephone the client for purposes such as appointment cancellations or reminders, or to give/receive other information, efforts are made to preserve confidentiality. Please list where we may reach you by phone and how you would like us to identify ourselves. For example, you might request that when we phone you at home or work, we do not say the name of the clinic or the nature of the call, but rather the mental health professional's first name only.

If this information is not provided to us (below), we will adhere to the following procedure when making phone calls: First we will ask to speak to the client (or guardian) without identifying the name of the clinic. If the person answering the phone asks for more identifying information we will say that it is a personal call. We will not identify the clinic (to protect confidentiality). If we reach an answering machine or voice mail we will follow the same guidelines.

PLEASE CHECK PLACES IN WHICH YOU MAY BE REACHED BY PHONE. Include phone numbers and how you would like us to identify ourselves when phoning you.

___ HOME   _____   _____   ___ Yes   ___ No

            Phone number   How should we identify ourselves?   May we say the clinic name?

___ WORK   _____   _____   ___ Yes   ___ No

            Phone number   How should we identify ourselves?   May we say the clinic name?

___ OTHER   _____   _____   ___ Yes   ___ No

            Phone number   How should we identify ourselves?   May we say the clinic name?

I agree to the above limits of confidentiality and understand their meanings and ramifications.

_____   _____   _____

Client's Name (please print)   Client's (or Guardian's) Signature   Date

Preauthorization for Health Care Form

Charge cards are an effective means of collecting fees for professional services. The following form provides several benefits (see page 1.20). It allows the clinic to automatically bill the charge-card company for third-party payments not received after a set number of (often 60) days. It eliminates expensive—and often ineffective—billing to the client and successive billing to the insurance company. It further allows the clinic to bill the charge-card company for recurring amounts such as co-payments. This policy is often welcomed by clients because it eliminates the need to write a check each time services are received.

Most banks offer both VISA and MasterCard dealer status, but established credit is needed. Some therapists have become vendors for credit-card companies by offering to back the funds with a secured interest-bearing account (e.g., $500) for a set period while their credit becomes established with the bank.

Fees for being a charge-card dealer vary and may be negotiated, so competitive shopping for a bank is suggested. Some banks charge a set percentage of each transaction, while others include several hidden fees. The process is simpler though when the same bank is used in which the mental health professional has a checking account, because charge account receipts are generally deposited into a checking account.

Preauthorization for Health Care

I authorize (Name of Clinic or mental health provider) to keep my signature on file and to charge my

_____ _Discover_____ account for:
                    (type of charge card)

_X_ All balances not paid by insurance or other third-party payers after 60 days. This total amount can not exceed $_500.00__ .

_X_ Recurring charges (ongoing treatment) as per amounts stated in the signed Payment Contract for Services with this clinic.

I assign my insurance benefits to the provider listed above. I understand that this form is valid for one year unless I cancel the authorization through written notice to this clinic.

_____*Judy Doe*_____
Client's Name

_____*Judy Doe*_____
Cardholder's Name

_*123 Main St.*_____
Cardholder's Billing Address

_*Pleasantville*_____   _*NJ*_____   _*99999*_____
City   State   Zip Code

_*1234-5678-9012-3456*_____   _*8-00*_____
Charge Card Number   Expiration Date

_*Judy Doe*_____   _*3-8-97*_____
Cardholder's Signature   Date

Preauthorization for Health Care

I authorize (_____) to keep my signature on file and to charge my

_____ account for:
　　　　　　　　(type of charge card)

___ All balances not paid by insurance or other third-party payers after 60 days. This total amount can not exceed $_____.

___ Recurring charges (ongoing treatment) as per amounts stated in the signed Payment Contract for Services with this clinic.

I assign my insurance benefits to the provider listed above. I understand that this form is valid for one year unless I cancel the authorization through written notice to this clinic.

_____
Client's Name

_____
Cardholder's Name

_____
Cardholder's Billing Address

_____　　_____　　_____
City　　　　　　　　　　　　　　　　　State　　　　　　　　　　Zip Code

_____　　_____
Charge Card Number　　　　　　　　　　　　　　　　Expiration Date

_____　　_____
Cardholder's Signature　　　　　　　　　　　　　　　Date

Release of Information Consent Form

The Release of Information Consent Form incorporates both legal and ethical obligations between the mental health professional and the client (see page 1.23). No information about clients should be discussed with anyone without that person's written permission, except information listed in the Limits of Confidentiality form (e.g., suicide, abuse, and so forth). A violation of confidentiality could lead to ethical, professional, and legal problems.

Clients have the right to know how the information will be used and which files will be released. A release of information is valid for one year, but may be cancelled at any time.

The legal guardians of children must sign the release. No release is necessary for children who are emancipated. It is necessary to find out if a vulnerable adult has a designated guardian (e.g., state or private guardianship, family).

The following release form allows for a two-way release of information (to and from various providers). Some agencies and some clients prefer to fill out a separate release for each transaction.

Release of Information Consent Form

I, _Judy Doe_____, authorize _(name of Clinic or Therapist)_____

to: ___ (send) __X__ (receive) the following ___ (to) __X__ (from) the following agencies or people:

Dr. Edward Benlingdon	_22 S Jackson St_	_Milltonberg_	_NJ_	_99889_	_987-6543_
Name	Address	City	State	Zip	Phone
Name	Address	City	State	Zip	Phone
Name	Address	City	State	Zip	Phone

( ) Academic Testing Results   ( ) Psychological Testing Results
( ) Behavior Programs   ( ) Service Plans
( ) Case Notes   ( ) Summary Reports
( ) Intelligence Testing Results   ( ) Vocational Testing Results
( ) Medical Reports   ( ) Entire Record
( ) Personality Profiles   ( ) Other (specify) _____
( ) Progress Reports   _____
(X) Psychological Reports   _____

The above information will be used for the following purposes:

( ) Planning Appropriate Treatment or Program
( ) Continuing Appropriate Treatment or Program
( ) Determining Eligibility for Benefits or Program
(X) Case Review
( ) Updating Files
( ) Other (specify) _____

I understand that I may revoke this consent at any time by providing written notice, and after one year this consent automatically expires. I have been informed what information will be given, its purpose, and who will receive the information.

Signature of Client _Judy Doe_____ Date _3-8-97_

Signature of Parent/Guardian _____ Date_____

Signature of Witness _____ Date_____
(if client is unable to sign)

Signature of Person Informing _Darlene L. Benton, Ph.D._____ Date _3-8-97_
Client of Rights

Mail to

Release of Information Consent Form

I, _____ , authorize _____

to: ___ (send)   ___ (receive) the following   ___ (to)   ___ (from) the following agencies or people:

_____
Name   Address   City   State   Zip   Phone

_____
Name   Address   City   State   Zip   Phone

_____
Name   Address   City   State   Zip   Phone

( ) Academic Testing Results   ( ) Psychological Testing Results
( ) Behavior Programs   ( ) Service Plans
( ) Case Notes   ( ) Summary Reports
( ) Intelligence Testing Results   ( ) Vocational Testing Results
( ) Medical Reports   ( ) Entire Record
( ) Personality Profiles   ( ) Other (specify) _____
( ) Progress Reports
( ) Psychological Reports   _____

                                       _____

The above information will be used for the following purposes:

( ) Planning Appropriate Treatment or Program
( ) Continuing Appropriate Treatment or Program
( ) Determining Eligibility for Benefits or Program
( ) Case Review
( ) Updating Files
( ) Other (specify) _____

I understand that I may revoke this consent at any time by providing written notice, and after one year this consent automatically expires. I have been informed what information will be given, its purpose, and who will receive the information.

Signature of Client _____ Date_____

Signature of Parent/Guardian _____ Date_____

Signature of Witness _____ Date_____
(if client is unable to sign)

Signature of Person Informing _____ Date_____
Client of Rights

Mail to

Discharge
Summary
Form

The discharge summary is a brief checklist indicating why services were terminated with the client and the effectiveness of the therapy (see page 1.26).

Discharge Summary

Client's Name: _Judy Doe_ Therapist: _DLB_

Date of Admission: _3-8-97_ Date of Discharge: _10-12-97_

Reason Terminated:

_X_ Service Plan Objectives Completed

___ Service Plan Objectives Not Completed (other appropriate services not available)

___ Agency Terminated Client Due to Noncooperation

___ Client Referred to Another Agency

___ Client Terminated Against Recommendation of Agency

___ Client Deceased

___ Client Moved

___ Client Incarcerated

___ Other: _____

Discharge Primary Diagnosis: _296.32 Major Depression, mild, recurrent, in remission_

Discharge Secondary Diagnosis: _____

Referred to: _____ Number of Visits: _____

Discharge Summary: _Client has met 80% of treatment goals. Reports significant improvements in occupational and social functioning. Feeling much more comfortable about role as teacher. Substantial increases in social contacts. Has missed no work in past 30 days. Decreased self-blame. Ongoing concerns with fatigue; continues visits with psychiatrist for med management. Sleeping patterns stabilizing at acceptable level._

Darlene L. Benton, Ph.D. _10-21-97_

Therapist Date

Sharon Bell, Ph.D. _10-21-97_

Supervisor Date

Discharge Summary

Client's Name: _____   Therapist: _____

Date of Admission: _____   Date of Discharge: _____

Reason Terminated:
___   Service Plan Objectives Completed
___   Service Plan Objectives Not Completed (other appropriate services not available)
___   Agency Terminated Client Due to Noncooperation
___   Client Referred to Another Agency
___   Client Terminated Against Recommendation of Agency
___   Client Deceased
___   Client Moved
___   Client Incarcerated
___   Other: _____

Discharge Primary Diagnosis: _____

Discharge Secondary Diagnosis: _____

Referred to: _____   Number of Visits: _____

Discharge Summary: _____
_____
_____
_____
_____
_____

_____   _____
Therapist   Date

_____   _____
Supervisor   Date

1.27

Chapter 2

Assessment for Counseling Forms and Procedures

Intake Notes

Intake notes are taken during the initial meeting with the client. The goal of the first session is to establish and document a diagnosis, identify functional impairments, and determine respective onsets, frequencies, durations, intensities, and examples of DSM-IV (*Diagnostic and Statistical Manual of Mental Disorders*, 4th ed.) symptoms and impairments. Statements comparing current to previous functioning are also helpful.

Information Needed

Although intake procedures vary among professions, the following information should be obtained as a minimum.

Referral source

Presenting problem

Treatment history

Medical history/concerns/medications

Family/developmental/background information

Relationship history

Substance usage

Career history

Symptoms, including onset, frequency, duration, and intensity

Current affective state

Mental status

Specific issues

Desired outcomes

Motivation for change

Motivation for client cooperation

Intake information drives (provides necessary information for) the treatment plan and validates the diagnosis. Unless the intake material sufficiently supports a diagnosis according to DSM, it is vulnerable to rejection by a third party. The specific functional impairments documented in the intake material may include social, family, occupational, affective, physical, cognitive, sexual, educational, biopsychological, and other areas of impairment which support the diagnosis.

Treatment, according to several third-party criteria, becomes the process of alleviating functional impairments. Documentation is generally requested to be in behavioral terms (usually quantifiable, observable, or measurable). Thus, intake notes should specifically list baseline rates of behaviors for later comparisons of progress and setbacks. Baseline rates are also needed to help determine objective discharge criteria.

JUDY DOE. Judy Doe's intake notes list both background and current information about the client. Both types of information are necessary for therapy, but oservations regarding the current functional impairments are more needed for third-party documentation and accountability procedures. The Intake Notes form for Judy Doe on page 2.5 contains the therapist's documentation statements, such as the following:

> Psychomotor retardation, slumped posture. Appeared depressed. Slow, soft speech. . . . Blunted affect. . . . Depressed 3 out of 4 days. . . . Does not want to spend time with former friends with whom she previously socialized 1–2 evenings/week. Missing 2–4 days of work per month. Previously . . . 1 day per year. . . . Takes 2–3 hours to fall asleep . . . wakes up 3–4 times per night. . . . Activities that were once pleasurable are no longer enjoyable.

Judy Doe's intake statement helps to document a diagnosis, describe the client's mental health condition, provide a baseline for certain depressive behaviors, and reflect current issues to be dealt with in therapy.

Intake Notes

1) CLIENT: _Judy Doe_   2) DATE: _3-8-97_

                      3) SOURCE OF

4) INTAKE THERAPIST: _Darlene L. Benton, Ph.D._   REFERRAL: _Yellow pages_

5) TYPE(S) OF COUNSELING: _X_ Individual ___Family ___Group ___Other _____

6) PRESENTING PROBLEM: _Self-referred, depressed mood, marital conflict, low motivation, feels stressed._

7) COUNSELING HISTORY: PRESENT COUNSELING __Y _X_N   PREVIOUS COUNSELING _X_Y __N

Purpose	Counselor	When	Duration	Outcome
Depression	DK	1967	1 year	Helpful

8) MEDICAL CONCERNS/Rx: _Describes self as being in generally good health, but recent fatigue and headaches. No medications at this time. Recent poor appetite and weight loss of 20# in past year._

9) FAMILY HISTORY (of origin): _#2 of 5 children. Describes family relationships in positive terms. No noted abuse. Father now deceased. Possible alcoholism with father. Both parents worked full-time. Notes that mother took care of everything ... hard to live up to mother's standards, even today. Presently receiving much unwanted advice from mother and older brother, but, "it would not be nice to be rude to them." No known family mental health issues._

10) MARITAL/RELATIONSHIP Hx: _Began dating at age 15 (secretly, against mother's wishes). Most dating relationships lasted about 1–2 years after which the other person broke off the relationship. In college broke up with a man she "loved dearly." Breakup led to depression and missed one term of college. Dated present spouse 6 months, now married 20 years (1st marriage). Upset that she "does all of the work and no one appreciates me." Desires to remain in marriage, but "sad that no one cares."_

11) SUBSTANCE USE/ABUSE Hx: _Denies previous or current alcohol/drug dependence. Occasional social drinking on holidays._

12) CAREER/EDUCATIONAL Hx: _Worked full-time during college to help support aging parents. Has worked in present teaching position since shortly after college graduation. Currently very dissatisfied with career. "I can't do anything right anymore. ... what's the use?"_

13) **RECENT AFFECTIVE STATE:** _Depressed mood. Little motivation. Forces self to perform_
minimal tasks. Little energy at work and home; fatigued. Low ego strength. Increased
crying spells (often 3–4x/day "for no reason at all"). Increased withdrawal into her bedroom.
"I don't feel like doing anything anymore."

14) **MENTAL STATUS:** _Oriented x3. No evidence of a thought disorder. In touch with reality._
Able to maintain conversation. Suicidal ideation at times, no plan, no Hx of suicidality.
Psychomotor retardation, slumped posture. Appeared depressed. Slow, soft speech. Submissive.
Blunted affect. Difficulty making decisions.

15) **SPECIFIC CONCERNS** (Include functional impairments/strengths; social, affective, occupational, legal, educational, physical)

1 _Depressed 3 out of 4 days. Often crying "for no reason at all." Does not want to spend_
2 _time with former friends with whom she previously socialized 1–2 evenings/week. Increased_
3 _irritability has harmed friendships and marital relationship. Believes that marital and_
4 _occupational problems are her fault. Now avoiding most significant others because they_
5 _say she is too irritable and edgy. Missing 2–4 days of work per month. Previously missed_
6 _about 1 day per year. "Too tired, too upset, too washed up." Increased lack of sleep. Takes 2–3_
7 _hours to fall asleep. Usually awakens at 3:00 to 4:00 a.m., often wakes up 3–4 times per night._
8 _"I don't teach like I used to." Activities that were once pleasurable are no longer enjoyable._
9 _Quite concerned about no one listening to her or helping her out. She doesn't understand why_
10 _she must do "everything for everybody." Viewing life as quite unfair to her, but not to others_
11 _she knows. Notes having difficulties expressing her frustrations re how other people don't_
12 _appreciate her. "Sad" and blames self that she "cannot motivate anyone to get things done."_
13 _Has come to counseling because she wants to return to previous level of affective functioning._
14
15
16
17
18
19
20

(Note: If additional space is needed use a case notes sheet)

TESTS/HANDOUTS/ASSIGNMENTS GIVEN: _Biographical information form_

TIME STARTED: _2:00_   **TIME FINISHED:** _2:52_   **DURATION:** _1 hour_
NEXT APPOINTMENT: _3-15-97_

Therapist's Signature _Darlene L. Benton, Ph.D._   Date _3-8-97_

Intake Notes

1) CLIENT:_____ 2) DATE: _____
   _____ 3) SOURCE OF
4) INTAKE THERAPIST: _____   REFERRAL:_____
5) TYPE(S) OF COUNSELING: ___Individual ___Family ___Group ___Other _____
6) PRESENTING PROBLEM: _____
   _____
7) COUNSELING HISTORY: PRESENT COUNSELING __Y __N   PREVIOUS COUNSELING __Y __N

Purpose	Counselor	When	Duration	Outcome
_____	_____	_____	_____	_____
_____	_____	_____	_____	_____
_____	_____	_____	_____	_____

8) MEDICAL CONCERNS/Rx: _____
   _____
   _____
   _____

9) FAMILY HISTORY (of origin):
   _____
   _____
   _____
   _____
   _____
   _____
   _____
   _____

10) MARITAL/RELATIONSHIP Hx:_____
    _____
    _____
    _____
    _____
    _____

11) SUBSTANCE USE/ABUSE Hx:_____
    _____
    _____
    _____
    _____

12) CAREER/EDUCATIONAL Hx: _____
    _____
    _____

13) RECENT AFFECTIVE STATE:

_____

_____

_____

_____

_____

14) MENTAL STATUS: _____

_____

_____

_____

_____

_____

_____

_____

15) SPECIFIC CONCERNS (Include functional impairments/strengths; social, affective, occupational, legal, educational, physical)

1 _____
2 _____
3 _____
4 _____
5 _____
6 _____
7 _____
8 _____
9 _____
10 _____
11 _____
12 _____
13 _____
14 _____
15 _____
16 _____
17 _____
18 _____
19 _____
20 _____

(Note: If additional space is needed use a case notes sheet)

TESTS/HANDOUTS/ASSIGNMENTS GIVEN: _____

_____

_____

TIME STARTED: _____ TIME FINISHED: _____ DURATION: _____

NEXT APPOINTMENT: _____

Five Sources of Information Available from the Intake Session(s)

The mental health intake procedure serves several purposes, including rapport building, information gathering, diagnosis, and setting up the treatment plan, each of which is necessary for accurate documentation. Information is available from at least five sources, including:

1. Diagnostic interview and mental status examination (observations by the clinician).
2. Testing (standardized, objective measures).
3. Self-report information (questionnaires filled out by the client).
4. Historical documents (past behaviors).
5. Collateral information (other people involved in the client's life).

1. THE DIAGNOSTIC INTERVIEW AND MENTAL STATUS EXAMINATION. The diagnostic interview is subject to limitations of validity and reliability. It is as valid as the diagnostic category. Some diagnoses have clear DSM-IV criteria and are more easily identified than others. For example, a major depressive episode is clearly defined in the DSM-IV; but several other disorders seem to be less clearly defined, causing the differential diagnosis to be more tentative and less valid.

The interview is as reliable as the clinician's knowledge of psychopathology. A vague knowledge of DSM-IV symptomology and differential diagnoses limits specificity, leading to erratic treatment. Mental health professionals can increase the reliability of their diagnoses by increasing their knowledge of psychopathology.

The interview should clearly document the onset, frequency, duration, and intensity of each symptom. Without this information there would be problems in differential diagnosis. For example, a diagnosis of dysthymic disorder cannot be given unless the person has been depressed for at least two years. Without documentation of a history of depression for this time period, dysthymia is not adequately documented. In this example, a misdiagnosis could lead to improper treatment. Treatment for dysthymia is not the same as treatment for other types of depression such as single-episode major depression, bipolar disorder, or an adjustment disorder with depressed mood.

2. TESTING. It is the clinician's responsibility to choose tests that are valid measures of the behaviors in question. That is, the test must measure what it purports to measure. Some clinics have been known to administer the same battery of tests to all clients, whatever the reason for therapy or evaluation. Some mental health professionals were able to get away with such unscrupulous billing a few years ago, but current contracts with third-party payers stipulate that if a test is administered there must be documented verification that the information derived for the particular test is medically necessary for accurate treatment. Clients should be informed that services such as testing or other procedures may not be covered by third-party payers. Payment contracts and financial policies should cover such provisions.

Standardized testing may be used as a documentation procedure in at least three ways: norm-referenced, criterion-referenced, and self-referenced. The same test can be used for all three purposes.

In norm-referenced testing, a person's test performance is compared with a normal population or a reference group. Most test distributions follow a normal curve in which the greatest number of people score at the 50th percentile and increasingly fewer people's scores approach the extremes. Scores are generally reported as standard scores. For example most intelligence tests (e.g., Wechsler Adult Intelligence Scale—Revised [WAIS-R]) have a mean of 100 (i.e., average intelligence quotient [IQ] = 100) and a standard deviation of 15. Approximately 68 percent of test takers score within one standard deviation from the mean

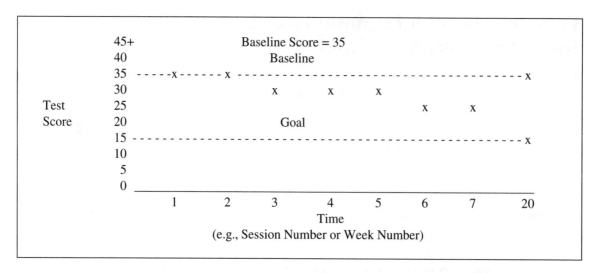

Figure 2.1   Graph of Therapeutic Progress Using Self-Referenced Testing.

(i.e., 68 percent of the population have an IQ between 85 and 115). Increasingly fewer people score higher or lower if the test follows a normal curve.

Criterion-referenced testing involves setting cutoff scores based on diagnostic categories. Referring to the previous example, WAIS-R criterion scores have been set as follows:

Standard Score (IQ)	Category
69 and below	Mentally retarded or mentally deficient
70–79	Borderline
80–89	Low average
90–109	Average
110–119	High average
120–129	Superior
130 and above	Very superior

In self-referenced testing, an individual's test scores are compared over time. For example, some therapists ask clients to fill out a brief test periodically (e.g., Beck Depression Inventory). Scores are charted throughout therapy and progress is measured by affective changes depicted by test scores. Self-referenced testing could be charted as in Figure 2.1.

3. SELF-REPORT INFORMATION. Additional information may be obtained by asking the client to fill out a biographical information form either prior to the initial interview or after the intake session (and returned prior to the second session). This information is especially helpful because the client is able to spend sufficient time in private delineating various historical, familial, medical, and mental health concerns. Also, using simple graphs such as those depicted in Figure 2.2, the client can furnish examples of impairment involving a wide range of mental health and behavioral symptoms. The information provided converts to treatment plan objectives.

4. HISTORICAL DOCUMENTS. Reports and evaluations by other professionals are quite helpful in documenting the client's mental health history. These are generally obtained from other professionals, schools, and agencies or, at times, brought in by the client. They must be requested in writing and the request form signed by the client. (See Release of Information Consent Form on page 1.23.)

5. COLLATERAL INFORMATION. Collateral information is data disclosed by others in the assessment session. For example, a parent might supply background information about a child, or a stroke victim's spouse might provide information about functioning before and after the stroke.

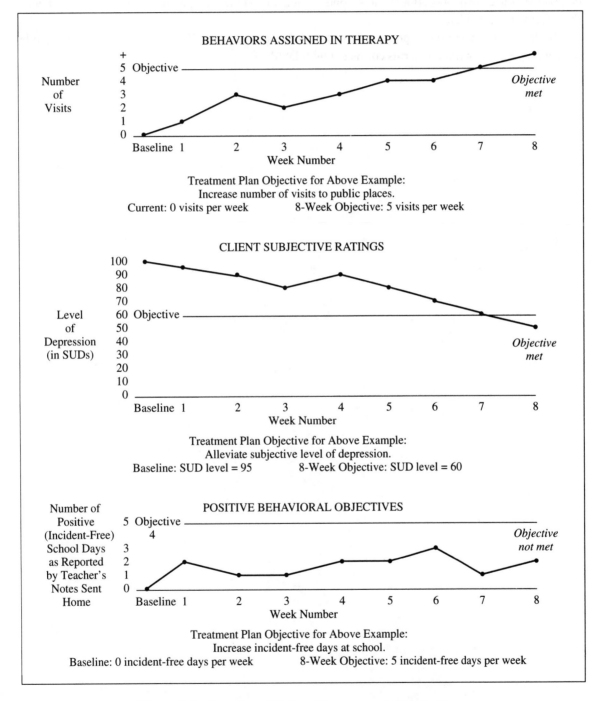

Figure 2.2 Samples of Various Documentation Techniques.

Biographical Information

A biographical information form is an effective means of documenting material not fully covered in the intake session. It is suggested that the client return this information to the therapist within a few days and before the second session. The first session (intake session) is intended to elicit specific diagnostic information. The second session (treatment planning session) is designed to collaboratively agree on the treatment plan with the client. Clients are given this form during the first session and asked to have it completed at least two days prior to the second session so that the therapist has sufficient time to review the information provided.

Both child and adult biographical information forms are provided. The child version is filled out by the parents. Each is written in terms consistent with DSM-IV.

Biographical Information Form— Adult

The Biographical Information Form (see page 2.15) asks clients to provide a wide range of information such as personal, counseling, medical, and family history. The relative importance of this information often depends on the therapist's frame of reference. Page 2.19 lists specific DSM-IV–related thoughts and behaviors for which the client rates the degree of concern. The client is further asked to comment on impairing concerns taking place frequently. The section on page 2.20 titled "Symptoms" is modeled after the DSM-IV. Page 2.21 gives the client an opportunity to list strengths and weaknesses and specific difficulties needing interventions.

Judy Doe

The Biographical Information Form filled out by Judy Doe documents her diagnosis and provides additional information for treatment planning. Examples of important diagnostic information provided by Judy Doe in her Biographical Information Form are as follows:

BIF Line #	Answer Provided by Client
20	Previously in counseling for depression
22	Depressed for the past year, but historical depression
30	Good health
35	No medications
69	Notes frequent occurrence of the following thoughts:

Life is hopeless.	I want to die.
I am lonely.	I can't concentrate.
No one cares about me.	I am so depressed.
I am a failure.	I have no emotions.

70   Endorses the following symptoms/impairments:

Avoiding people	Sexual difficulties
Depression	Sick often
Distractibility	Sleeping problems
Fatigue	Suicidal thoughts
Hopelessness	Withdrawing
Loneliness	Worrying

The Biographical Information Form is written in DSM-IV terminology and designed to validate diagnostic criteria and subsequent impairments. As in the intake session, the information is incorporated into the treatment plan and subsequent interventions.

Biographical Information Form—Adult

Instructions: To assist us in helping you, please fill out this form as fully and openly as possible. All private information is held in strictest confidence within legal limits. If certain questions do not apply to you, leave them blank.

Personal History

1) Name: _Judy Doe_ 2) Age: _48_ 3) Gender: __M _X_ F
4) Address: _1234 Main St._ _Plasantville_ _NJ_ _99999_
    Street & Number   City   State   Zip
5) Weight: _148_ 6) Height: _5-3_ 7) Eye color: _Bl_ 8) Hair color: _Br_ 9) Race: _Cau_
10) Today's Date: _3-12-97_ 11) Date of Birth: _7-6-48_ 12) Years of education: _16_
13) Occupation: _Teacher_ 14) Home Phone: _555-5555_ 15) Business Phone: _555-5544_
16) Present Marital Status:

_____	1) never married	_____	5) separated
_____	2) engaged to be married	_____	6) divorced and not remarried
_X_	3) married now for first time	_____	7) widowed and not remarried
_____	4) married now after first time	_____	8) other (specify) _____

17) If married, are you living with your spouse at present?: Yes _X_ No____
18) If married, years married to present spouse: ____20____

Counseling History

19) Are you receiving counseling services at present?: Yes____ No _X_
    If Yes, please briefly describe: _____
    _____

20) Have you received counseling in the past?: Yes _X_ No_____
    If Yes, please briefly describe: _In 1968 when in college I had a stressful_
    relationship breakup. I went through therapy for about one year for depression.

21) What is (are) your main reason(s) for this visit?: _I am depressed. I just don't_
    care about things at home or at work.
    _____

22) How long has this problem persisted (from #21)?: _Mainly in the past year,_
    but I've been this way before in my life.

23) Under what conditions do your problems usually get worse?: _When there are_
    too many demands placed on me.

24) Under what conditions are your problems usually improved?: _When I'm alone._
    _____

25) How did you hear about this clinic, or who referred you?: _Yellow pages_
    _____

Medical History

26) Name and address of your primary physician:
Physician's name: _____ *Dr. Hope Wellby* _____
Address: _____ *The Clinic* _____

27) List any major illnesses and/or operations you have had: _____ *None* _____

28) List any physical concerns you are having at present: (e.g., high blood pressure, headaches,
dizziness, etc.): _____ *Occasional headaches* _____

29) List any other physical concerns you have experienced in the past: _____ *None* _____

30) When was your most recent complete physical exam?: _____ *5 years ago* _____
Results of physical exam: _____ *good health* _____

31) On average how many hours of sleep do you get daily?: _____ *5* _____

32) Do you have trouble falling asleep at night?: __No X Yes If Yes, describe _____ *It often*
takes a few hours just to fall asleep. I don't know why. _____

33) Have you gained/lost over ten pounds in the past year?: X Yes __No, __gained X lost
If Yes, was the gain/loss on purpose?: __Yes X No

34) Describe your appetite (during the past week):
__X__ poor appetite   _____ average appetite   _____ large appetite

35) What medications (and dosages) are you taking at present, and for what purpose?:
Medication   Purpose
None _____   _____

Religious Concerns

36) What is your present religious affiliation?:
___ 1) Catholic
___ 2) Jewish
___ 3) Protestant (specify denomination if any) _____
_X_ 4) None, but I believe in God
___ 5) Atheist or agnostic
___ 6) Other (please specify) _____

37) How important is religious commitment to you?:

Unimportant			Average importance			Extremely important
1	2	3	4	5	6	7

38) Do you desire to have your religious beliefs and values incorporated into the counseling process?:
__Yes X No __Not sure   (If Yes, please explain) _____

Family History

39) Mother's age: _71_ If deceased, how old were you when she died?: _____

40) Father's age: _Deceased_ If deceased, how old were you when he died?: _____39_____

41) If your parents are separated or divorced, how old were you then?: _____

42) Number of brother(s) _2_ Their ages _51_ _42_ ____ ____ ____ ____

43) Number of sister(s) _2_ Their ages _46_ _44_ ____ ____ ____ ____

44) I was child number _2_ in a family of _5_ children.

45) Were you adopted or raised with parents other than your natural parents?: Yes___ No _X_

46) Briefly describe your relationship with your brothers and/or sisters: _____

We got along well. Typical family ups and downs.

47) Which of the following best describes the family in which you grew up?:

WARM AND ACCEPTING				AVERAGE				HOSTILE AND FIGHTING
1	(2)	3	4	5	6	7	8	9

48) Which of the following best describes the way in which your family raised you?:

ALLOWED ME TO BE VERY INDEPENDENT				AVERAGE				ATTEMPTED TO CONTROL ME
1	2	3	4	5	6	(7)	8	9

YOUR MOTHER (or mother substitute)

49) Briefly describe your mother: _Kind, giving, did too much for others._

50) How did she discipline you?: _Sent me to my room and lectured me._

51) How did she reward you?: _Go shopping, extra allowance money._

52) How much time did she spend with you when you were a child?: _____
_____ much _X_ average _____ little

53) Your mother's occupation when you were a child: _Worked in a bakery_
_____ stayed home _____ worked outside part-time _X_ worked outside full-time

54) How did you get along with your mother when you were a child?:
_____ poorly _____ average _X_ well

55) How do you get along with your mother now?:
_____ poorly _____ average _X_ well

2.17

56) Did your mother have any problems (e.g., alcoholism, violence, etc.) that may have affected your childhood development?: Yes _____ No __X____
(If Yes, please describe) _____
_____

57) Is there anything unusual about your relationship with your mother?:
Yes _____ No __X____ (If Yes, please describe) _____
_____

58) Describe overall how your mother treated the following people as you were growing up:
(Circle one answer for each)

YOUR MOTHER'S TREATMENT OF:	Poor			Average			Excellent
1) YOU	1	2	3	4	5	⑥	7
2) YOUR FAMILY	1	2	3	4	5	⑥	7
3) YOUR FATHER	1	2	3	4	5	⑥	7

YOUR FATHER (or father substitute)

59) Briefly describe your father: _____ *Fun, but stern* _____
_____

60) How did he discipline you?: _____ *Light spanking or grounded* _____
_____

61) How did he reward you?: _____ *Money, toys, dolls, etc.* _____
_____

62) How much time did he spend with you when you were a child?:
_____ much __X__ average _____ little

63) Your father's occupation when you were a child:_____ *TV repairman* ___
_____ stayed home _____ worked outside part-time __X__ worked outside full-time

64) How did you get along with your father when you were a child?: _____
_____ poorly _____ average __X__ well

65) How do you get along with your father now?:
_____ poorly _____ average __X__ well

66) Did your father have any problems (e.g. alcoholism, violence, etc.) that may have affected your childhood development?: Yes__?___ No__?____
(If Yes, please describe) _____ *Drank socially on weekends. May have been intoxicated at times* ____

67) Is there anything unusual about your relationship with your father?: No __X__ Yes _____
(If Yes, please describe) _____
_____

68) Describe overall how your father treated the following people as you were growing up:
(Circle one answer for each)

YOUR FATHER'S TREATMENT OF:	Poor			Average			Excellent
1) YOU	1	2	3	4	5	6	⑦
2) YOUR FAMILY	1	2	3	4	5	6	⑦
3) YOUR MOTHER	1	2	3	4	5	6	⑦

Thoughts and Behaviors

69) Please check how often the following thoughts occur to you:

1)	Life is hopeless.	____Never	____Rarely	____Sometimes	_X_ Frequently
2)	I am lonely.	____Never	____Rarely	____Sometimes	_X_ Frequently
3)	No one cares about me.	____Never	____Rarely	____Sometimes	_X_ Frequently
4)	I am a failure.	____Never	____Rarely	____Sometimes	_X_ Frequently
5)	Most people don't like me.	____Never	____Rarely	_X_ Sometimes	____Frequently
6)	I want to die.	____Never	____Rarely	____Sometimes	_X_ Frequently
7)	I want to hurt someone.	____Never	_X_ Rarely	____Sometimes	____Frequently
8)	I am so stupid.	____Never	____Rarely	_X_ Sometimes	____Frequently
9)	I am going crazy.	____Never	_X_ Rarely	____Sometimes	____Frequently
10)	I can't concentrate.	____Never	____Rarely	____Sometimes	_X_ Frequently
11)	I am so depressed.	____Never	____Rarely	____Sometimes	_X_ Frequently
12)	God is disappointed in me.	____Never	____Rarely	_X_ Sometimes	____Frequently
13)	I can't be forgiven.	____Never	____Rarely	_X_ Sometimes	____Frequently
14)	Why am I so different?	____Never	____Rarely	_X_ Sometimes	____Frequently
15)	I can't do anything right.	____Never	____Rarely	_X_ Sometimes	____Frequently
16)	People hear my thoughts.	_X_ Never	____Rarely	____Sometimes	____Frequently
17)	I have no emotions.	____Never	____Rarely	____Sometimes	_X_ Frequently
18)	Someone is watching me.	_X_ Never	____Rarely	____Sometimes	____Frequently
19)	I hear voices in my head.	_X_ Never	____Rarely	____Sometimes	____Frequently
20)	I am out of control.	_X_ Never	____Rarely	____Sometimes	____Frequently

Please comment (e.g., examples, frequency, duration, effects on you) about each of the above thoughts that occur frequently or are a concern to you. Use the back of this sheet if necessary.

I just don't care about anything. I don't want to be around others, go to work, or even get
up in the morning. When people ask me how I'm doing, I just want to say, "fine" and
find a place to hide. I'm a loser, so why should I try to get ahead? No one cares—they
just care about themselves. Maybe I should just quit teaching. What can people learn
from me? Usually I just feel nothing inside and don't care. Often I want to die, but
that's not right. It's like I'm around lots of people, but still alone. What's the use?

_____
_____
_____
_____
_____
_____
_____

Symptoms

70) Check the behaviors and symptoms that occur to you more often than you would like them to take place:

_____ aggression	__X__ fatigue	__X__ sexual difficulties
_____ alcohol dependence	_____ hallucinations	__X__ sick often
_____ anger	_____ heart palpitations	__X__ sleeping problems
_____ antisocial behavior	_____ high blood pressure	_____ speech problems
_____ anxiety	__X__ hopelessness	__X__ suicidal thoughts
__X__ avoiding people	_____ impulsivity	_____ thoughts disorganized
_____ chest pain	_____ irritability	_____ trembling
__X__ depression	_____ judgment errors	__X__ withdrawing
_____ disorientation	__X__ loneliness	__X__ worrying
__X__ distractibility	_____ memory impairment	_____ other (specify)
_____ dizziness	_____ mood shifts	_____
_____ drug dependence	_____ panic attacks	_____
_____ eating disorder	_____ phobias/fears	_____
_____ elevated mood	_____ recurring thoughts	

Please give examples of how each of the symptoms that you checked impairs your ability to function (e.g., socially, emotionally, occupationally, physically, etc.). Use the back of this sheet if necessary.

My friends are not visiting me. When my husband is upset I get down. I don't want to be around others because they know what a loser I am. Why am I always so sick and tired? I can't keep my mind on anything anymore. I no longer have any interest in sex. I worry all the time about money, people, and what is in the future. When I get too upset, I look for an argument. I'm sure I'll lose my job. I won't commit suicide, but no one would notice if I did. Lately, when I teach, I will be talking about a subject and forget what I have told the students and feel really stupid. Lately, I've gotten up in the morning and felt too sick to go to work.

71) List your five greatest strengths:
   1)   *Good provider*
   2)   *Religious beliefs*
   3)   *Honest*
   4)
   5)

72) List your five greatest weaknesses:
   1)   *Impatient*
   2)   *Hard to take much pressure*
   3)   *Give up too easily*
   4)   *Intolerant of other people's differences*
   5)

73) List your main social difficulties:
I don't feel like being around other people. I don't want to meet new people.
What do I have to offer?

74) List your main love and sex difficulties:
I have no interest in sex anymore. No one can make me happy. Why would
anyone love me? What do I have to offer? I feel no love toward my spouse.

75) List your main difficulties at school or work:
I used to enjoy teaching, but now I dread seeing students and colleagues.
Nothing happens. No one cares. I don't care either.

76) List your main difficulties at home:
Frustrated with husband because he treats me like a child. Children won't help
out and it's hard to keep up around the house.

77) List your behaviors that you would like to change:
Be more motivated, happy, and friendly (the way I used to be).

78) Additional information you believe would be helpful:
If this counseling doesn't help, I'll probably lose my job and marriage.
I'm going nowhere.

**PLEASE RETURN THIS AND OTHER ASSESSMENT MATERIALS TO THIS
OFFICE AT LEAST TWO DAYS BEFORE YOUR NEXT APPOINTMENT.**

Biographical Information Form—Adult

Instructions: To assist us in helping you, please fill out this form as fully and openly as possible. All private information is held in strictest confidence within legal limits. If certain questions do not apply to you, leave them blank.

Personal History

1) Name: _____ 2) Age: _____ 3) Gender: ___M ___F

4) Address: _____

                          Street & Number   City   State   Zip

5) Weight: _____ 6) Height: _____ 7) Eye color: _____ 8) Hair color: _____ 9) Race: _____

10) Today's Date: _____ 11) Date of Birth: _____ 12) Years of education: _____

13) Occupation: _____ 14) Home Phone: _____ 15) Business Phone: _____

16) Present Marital Status:

_____ 1) never married	_____ 5) separated
_____ 2) engaged to be married	_____ 6) divorced and not remarried
_____ 3) married now for first time	_____ 7) widowed and not remarried
_____ 4) married now after first time	_____ 8) other (specify) _____

17) If married, are you living with your spouse at present?: Yes____ No____

18) If married, years married to present spouse: _____

Counseling History

19) Are you receiving counseling services at present?: Yes____ No____

      If Yes, please briefly describe: _____

_____

20) Have you received counseling in the past?: Yes_____ No_____

      If Yes, please briefly describe: _____

_____

21) What is (are) your main reason(s) for this visit?: _____

_____

_____

22) How long has this problem persisted (from #21)?: _____

_____

23) Under what conditions do your problems usually get worse?: _____

_____

24) Under what conditions are your problems usually improved?: _____

_____

25) How did you hear about this clinic, or who referred you?: _____

_____

Medical History

26) Name and address of your primary physician:
Physician's name: _____
Address: _____

27) List any major illnesses and/or operations you have had: _____
_____

28) List any physical concerns you are having at present: (e.g., high blood pressure, headaches,
dizziness, etc.): _____
_____

29) List any other physical concerns you have experienced in the past: _____
_____
_____

30) When was your most recent complete physical exam?: _____
Results of physical exam: _____
_____

31) On average how many hours of sleep do you get daily?: _____

32) Do you have trouble falling asleep at night?: __No __Yes If Yes, describe _____
_____

33) Have you gained/lost over ten pounds in the past year?: __Yes __No, __gained __lost
If Yes, was the gain/loss on purpose?: __Yes __No

34) Describe your appetite (during the past week):
_____ poor appetite   _____ average appetite   _____ large appetite

35) What medications (and dosages) are you taking at present, and for what purpose?:
<u>Medication</u>   <u>Purpose</u>
_____   _____
_____   _____
_____   _____
_____   _____

Religious Concerns

36) What is your present religious affiliation?:
____ 1) Catholic
____ 2) Jewish
____ 3) Protestant (specify denomination if any) _____
____ 4) None, but I believe in God
____ 5) Atheist or agnostic
____ 6) Other (please specify) _____

37) How important is religious commitment to you?:

Unimportant			Average importance			Extremely important
1	2	3	4	5	6	7

38) Do you desire to have your religious beliefs and values incorporated into the counseling process?:
__Yes __No __Not sure   (If Yes, please explain) _____
_____

Family History

39) Mother's age:_____ If deceased, how old were you when she died?: _____

40) Father's age:_____ If deceased, how old were you when he died?: _____

41) If your parents are separated or divorced, how old were you then?: _____

42) Number of brother(s) _____ Their ages _____ _____ _____ _____ _____ _____

43) Number of sister(s) _____ Their ages _____ _____ _____ _____ _____ _____

44) I was child number _____ in a family of _____ children.

45) Were you adopted or raised with parents other than your natural parents?: Yes___ No ___

46) Briefly describe your relationship with your brothers and/or sisters: _____
_____
_____
_____

47) Which of the following best describes the family in which you grew up?:

WARM AND								HOSTILE AND
ACCEPTING				AVERAGE				FIGHTING
1	2	3	4	5	6	7	8	9

48) Which of the following best describes the way in which your family raised you?:

ALLOWED ME								
TO BE VERY								ATTEMPTED TO
INDEPENDENT				AVERAGE				CONTROL ME
1	2	3	4	5	6	7	8	9

YOUR MOTHER (or mother substitute)

49) Briefly describe your mother: _____
_____

50) How did she discipline you?: _____
_____

51) How did she reward you?: _____
_____

52) How much time did she spend with you when you were a child?:_____
_____ much _____ average _____ little

53) Your mother's occupation when you were a child:_____

_____ stayed home _____ worked outside part-time _____ worked outside full-time

54) How did you get along with your mother when you were a child?:

_____ poorly _____ average _____ well

55) How do you get along with your mother now?:

_____ poorly _____ average _____ well

2.24

56) Did your mother have any problems (e.g., alcoholism, violence, etc.) that may have affected your childhood development?: Yes _____   No _____

(If Yes, please describe) _____

_____

57) Is there anything unusual about your relationship with your mother?:

Yes _____   No _____   (If Yes, please describe) _____

_____

58) Describe overall how your mother treated the following people as you were growing up:

(Circle one answer for each)

YOUR MOTHER'S TREATMENT OF:	Poor			Average			Excellent
1) YOU	1	2	3	4	5	6	7
2) YOUR FAMILY	1	2	3	4	5	6	7
3) YOUR FATHER	1	2	3	4	5	6	7

YOUR FATHER (or father substitute)

59) Briefly describe your father: _____

_____

60) How did he discipline you?: _____

_____

61) How did he reward you?: _____

_____

62) How much time did he spend with you when you were a child?:

_____ much   _____ average   _____ little

63) Your father's occupation when you were a child:_____

_____ stayed home   _____ worked outside part-time   _____ worked outside full-time

64) How did you get along with your father when you were a child?:_____

_____ poorly   _____ average   _____ well

65) How do you get along with your father now?:

_____ poorly   _____ average   _____ well

66) Did your father have any problems (e.g. alcoholism, violence, etc.) that may have affected your childhood development?:   Yes_____   No_____

(If Yes, please describe) _____

_____

67) Is there anything unusual about your relationship with your father?: No _____ Yes _____

(If Yes, please describe) _____

_____

68) Describe overall how your father treated the following people as you were growing up:

(Circle one answer for each)

YOUR FATHER'S TREATMENT OF:	Poor			Average			Excellent
1) YOU	1	2	3	4	5	6	7
2) YOUR FAMILY	1	2	3	4	5	6	7
3) YOUR MOTHER	1	2	3	4	5	6	7

Thoughts and Behaviors

69) Please check how often the following thoughts occur to you:

1) Life is hopeless.	____Never ____Rarely	____Sometimes	____Frequently
2) I am lonely.	____Never ____Rarely	____Sometimes	____Frequently
3) No one cares about me.	____Never ____Rarely	____Sometimes	____Frequently
4) I am a failure.	____Never ____Rarely	____Sometimes	____Frequently
5) Most people don't like me.	____Never ____Rarely	____Sometimes	____Frequently
6) I want to die.	____Never ____Rarely	____Sometimes	____Frequently
7) I want to hurt someone.	____Never ____Rarely	____Sometimes	____Frequently
8) I am so stupid.	____Never ____Rarely	____Sometimes	____Frequently
9) I am going crazy.	____Never ____Rarely	____Sometimes	____Frequently
10) I can't concentrate.	____Never ____Rarely	____Sometimes	____Frequently
11) I am so depressed.	____Never ____Rarely	____Sometimes	____Frequently
12) God is disappointed in me.	____Never ____Rarely	____Sometimes	____Frequently
13) I can't be forgiven.	____Never ____Rarely	____Sometimes	____Frequently
14) Why am I so different?	____Never ____Rarely	____Sometimes	____Frequently
15) I can't do anything right.	____Never ____Rarely	____Sometimes	____Frequently
16) People hear my thoughts.	____Never ____Rarely	____Sometimes	____Frequently
17) I have no emotions.	____Never ____Rarely	____Sometimes	____Frequently
18) Someone is watching me.	____Never ____Rarely	____Sometimes	____Frequently
19) I hear voices in my head.	____Never ____Rarely	____Sometimes	____Frequently
20) I am out of control.	____Never ____Rarely	____Sometimes	____Frequently

Please comment (e.g., examples, frequency, duration, effects on you) about each of the above thoughts that occur frequently or are a concern to you. Use the back of this sheet if necessary.

_____
_____
_____
_____
_____
_____
_____
_____
_____
_____
_____
_____
_____

Symptoms

70) Check the behaviors and symptoms that occur to you more often than you would like them to take place:

_____ aggression	_____ fatigue	_____ sexual difficulties
_____ alcohol dependence	_____ hallucinations	_____ sick often
_____ anger	_____ heart palpitations	_____ sleeping problems
_____ antisocial behavior	_____ high blood pressure	_____ speech problems
_____ anxiety	_____ hopelessness	_____ suicidal thoughts
_____ avoiding people	_____ impulsivity	_____ thoughts disorganized
_____ chest pain	_____ irritability	_____ trembling
_____ depression	_____ judgment errors	_____ withdrawing
_____ disorientation	_____ loneliness	_____ worrying
_____ distractibility	_____ memory impairment	_____ other (specify)
_____ dizziness	_____ mood shifts	_____
_____ drug dependence	_____ panic attacks	_____
_____ eating disorder	_____ phobias/fears	_____
_____ elevated mood	_____ recurring thoughts	_____

Please give examples of how each of the symptoms that you checked impairs your ability to function (e.g., socially, emotionally, occupationally, physically, etc.). Use the back of this sheet if necessary.

_____
_____
_____
_____
_____
_____
_____
_____
_____
_____
_____
_____
_____
_____
_____
_____
_____
_____
_____
_____
_____
_____
_____
_____

2.27

71) List your five greatest strengths:
   1) _____
   2) _____
   3) _____
   4) _____
   5) _____

72) List your five greatest weaknesses:
   1) _____
   2) _____
   3) _____
   4) _____
   5) _____

73) List your main social difficulties: _____
_____
_____

74) List your main love and sex difficulties: _____
_____
_____

75) List your main difficulties at school or work: _____
_____
_____

76) List your main difficulties at home: _____
_____
_____

77) List your behaviors that you would like to change: _____
_____
_____
_____

78) Additional information you believe would be helpful: _____
_____
_____
_____
_____
_____
_____
_____
_____

PLEASE RETURN THIS AND OTHER ASSESSMENT MATERIALS TO THIS OFFICE AT LEAST TWO DAYS BEFORE YOUR NEXT APPOINTMENT.

Biographical Information Form—Child

Similar to the adult biographical information form, the children's version (see page 2.30) initially elicits background data. Additional information such as developmental history is included. Page 2.34 of the form lists several DSM-IV impairments categorized by the following topics:

Items 1–9	Oppositional defiant disorder
Items 10–21	Conduct disorder
Items 22–36	Attention deficit hyperactivity disorder (ADHD)
Items 37–50	Various learning and mental health issues

Biographical Information Form—Child

Instructions: To assist us in helping your child, please fill out this form as fully and openly as possible. All private information is held in strictest confidence within legal limits. If certain questions do not apply to the child, leave them blank.

Information supplied by: _Lisa Watters_   Relationship: _Mother_

Personal History

1) Child's Name: _Christine Watters_   2) Age: _6_   3) Gender: __M X F

4) Weight: _64_   5) Height: _4-4_   6) Eye color: _Brn_   7) Hair color: _Blk_   8) Race: _Afr-Am_

9) Address ___4567 Hayward St._____Tacoma_____WA_____99889___
              Street & Number   City   State   Zip

10) Today's Date: _4-2-97_   11) Date of Birth: _3-6-91_

12) Home Phone: _555-8899_   13) Year in School _1st_

14) Has the child been involved in previous counseling?: ___ Yes X No
    If Yes, please describe: _____
    _____

15) Why is the child coming to counseling?: _Disruptive behaviors. ADHD._
    _Won't sit still. Needs to learn how to settle down._____
    _____

16) How long has this problem persisted (from #15)?: _About 3 years_

17) Under what conditions do the problems usually get worse?: _When she does_
    not get her way.

18) Under what conditions are the problems usually improved?: _When she is not_
    under any stress and things are calm.

Medical History

19) Name and Address of Physician(s):
    Physician's Name: _Dr. Shawn Rellings_
    Address: _45678 Hayward St._____Tacoma,_____WA_____99889___
              Street & Number   City   State   Zip
    Most Recent Physical Exam: _Last year_   Results: _Good health_
    _____

20) List any major illnesses and/or operations: _None_____
    _____
    _____

21) List any physical concerns occurring at present (e.g., high blood pressure, headaches, dizziness, etc.): _None_____
    _____

2.30

22) List any physical concerns (e.g., head trauma, seizures, etc.) experienced in the past:
None
_____

23) On average how many hours of sleep does the child receive daily?: _____ *9* _____

24) Does the child have trouble falling asleep at night? _X_ Yes ___No
If Yes, how long has this been a problem? _*3–4 years*_

25) Describe the child's appetite (during the past week):
_____ poor appetite _*X*_ average appetite _____ large appetite

26) What medications (and dosages) are being taken at present, and for what purpose?: _____
None
_____

Family History

27) Mother's age: _*32*_ If deceased, how old was the child when she passed away?: _____
28) Father's age: _*39*_ If deceased, how old was the child when he passed away?: _____
29) If parents are separated or divorced, how old was the child then?: _____
30) Number of brother(s) _*1*_ Their ages _*4*_ ____ ____ ____ ____ ____
31) Number of sister(s) _*1*_ Their ages _*10*_ ____ ____ ____ ____ ____
32) Child number _*2*_ being in a family of _*3*_ children.
33) Is the child adopted or raised with parents other than biological parents?: ___ Yes _X_ No
34) Briefly describe the child's relationship with brothers and/or sisters:
Biological siblings: _*Increasingly annoying them. Picks on little brother. Tattles on*_
*older sister all the time. Usually get along when supervised.*
_____

Step and/or half siblings: _____
_____
_____

Other: _____
_____
_____

35) What is the family relationship between the child and his/her custodial parents?
Check all that apply:
____ Single parent mother _____ Single parent father _____ Parents unmarried
_X_ Parents married, together ____ Parents divorced _____ Parents separated
____ With mother and stepfather ____ With father and stepmother
____ Child adopted ____ Other, describe _____

36) Is there a history or recent occurrence(s) of child abuse to this child? ____ Yes _X_ No
If Yes, which type(s) of abuse? ____ Verbal _____ Physical ____ Sexual
Comments: _____
_____

37) Parents' occupations: Mother _Home catalog business_ Father _Insurance sales_

38) Briefly describe the style of parenting used in the household: _Children are expected to_
    behave and obey their parents. When they don't listen or they disobey, they are sent to their
    room for about one hour. When they behave they are praised. We have set rules and
    do not "reason" with the children. But as they get older they will be given more
    liberties to learn responsibility.

Developmental History

39) Briefly describe any problems in the child's mother's pregnancy and/or childbirth:
    None

40) Please fill in when the following developmental milestones took place:

Behavior	Age began	Comments
Walking	13 months	It seemed like she ran before she walked.
Talking	20 months	Hasn't stopped since then.
Toilet trained	4 years	

41) List any drugs used by mother or father at time of conception, or by mother during pregnancy:

42) Please rate your opinion of the child's development (compared to others the same age) in the following areas:

	Below Average	About Average	Above Average
Social	X		
Physical		X	
Language		X	
Intellectual		X	
Emotional	X		

For each type of development that you rated above as *below* average, please describe current areas of concern. Be specific.

Social—Immature, often teased by classmates

Emotional—Temper tantrums when feeling too stressed

43) List the child's three greatest strengths:
1) _Enjoys sports_
2) _Good health_
3) _Wants to be good_

44) List the child's three greatest weaknesses or needed areas of improvement:
1) _Often refuses to do what she is asked_
2) _Won't pay attention_
3) _Schoolwork_

45) List the child's main difficulties at school:
1) _Making friends_
2) _Completing work_
3) _Sitting still_

46) List the child's main difficulties at home:
1) _Completing tasks_
2) _Going to bed_
3) _Hyperactive_

47) Briefly describe the child's friendships: _One best friend for past year. Has brought_ _people from school home, but friendships do not last very long. Teased by several_ _children at school._

48) What report card grades does the child usually receive?: _"Needs improvement."_
Have these changed lately?: ___ Yes   _X_ No   If Yes, how?: _____

49) Briefly describe the child's hobbies and interests: _Video games, coloring. Sometimes_ _will do puzzles with little brother. Loves playing outside._

50) Describe how the child is disciplined: _Sent to room. Loses privileges. Never_ _spanked._

51) For what reasons is the child disciplined? _Disobeying, not doing homework,_ _picking on sister._

Behaviors of Concern

52) Please check how often the following behaviors occur. Those occurring FREQUENTLY or of special concern may be described on the next page.

1) Loses temper easily	___Never	___Rarely	X Sometimes	___Frequently
2) Argues with adults	___Never	___Rarely	X Sometimes	___Frequently
3) Refuses adults' requests	___Never	___Rarely	X Sometimes	___Frequently
4) Deliberately annoys people	___Never	___Rarely	X Sometimes	___Frequently
5) Blames others for own mistakes	___Never	X Rarely	___Sometimes	___Frequently
6) Easily annoyed by others	___Never	___Rarely	X Sometimes	___Frequently
7) Angry/resentful	___Never	___Rarely	X Sometimes	___Frequently
8) Spiteful/vindictive	___Never	___Rarely	X Sometimes	___Frequently
9) Defiant	___Never	___Rarely	X Sometimes	___Frequently
10) Bullies/teases others	___Never	X Rarely	___Sometimes	___Frequently
11) Initiates fights	X Never	___Rarely	___Sometimes	___Frequently
12) Uses a weapon	X Never	___Rarely	___Sometimes	___Frequently
13) Physically cruel to people	X Never	___Rarely	___Sometimes	___Frequently
14) Physically cruel to animals	X Never	___Rarely	___Sometimes	___Frequently
15) Stealing	___Never	X Rarely	___Sometimes	___Frequently
16) Forced sexual activity	X Never	___Rarely	___Sometimes	___Frequently
17) Intentional arson	X Never	___Rarely	___Sometimes	___Frequently
18) Burglary	X Never	___Rarely	___Sometimes	___Frequently
19) "Cons" other people	___Never	X Rarely	___Sometimes	___Frequently
20) Runs away from home	X Never	___Rarely	___Sometimes	___Frequently
21) Truant at school	X Never	___Rarely	___Sometimes	___Frequently
22) Doesn't pay attention to details	___Never	___Rarely	X Sometimes	___Frequently
23) Several careless mistakes	___Never	___Rarely	X Sometimes	___Frequently
24) Does not listen when spoken to	___Never	___Rarely	X Sometimes	___Frequently
25) Doesn't finish chores/homework	___Never	___Rarely	X Sometimes	___Frequently
26) Difficulty organizing tasks	___Never	___Rarely	X Sometimes	___Frequently
27) Loses things	___Never	___Rarely	X Sometimes	___Frequently
28) Easily distracted	___Never	___Rarely	X Sometimes	___Frequently
29) Forgetful in daily activities	___Never	___Rarely	X Sometimes	___Frequently
30) Fidgety/squirmy	___Never	___Rarely	___Sometimes	X Frequently
31) Difficulty remaining seated	___Never	___Rarely	___Sometimes	X Frequently
32) Runs/climbs around excessively	___Never	___Rarely	___Sometimes	X Frequently
33) Difficulty playing quietly	___Never	___Rarely	___Sometimes	X Frequently
34) Hyperactive	___Never	___Rarely	___Sometimes	X Frequently
35) Difficulty awaiting turn	___Never	___Rarely	___Sometimes	X Frequently
36) Interrupts others	___Never	___Rarely	___Sometimes	X Frequently
37) Problems pronouncing words	___Never	X Rarely	___Sometimes	___Frequently
38) Poor grades in school	___Never	___Rarely	___Sometimes	X Frequently
39) Expelled from school	X Never	___Rarely	___Sometimes	___Frequently
40) Drug abuse	X Never	___Rarely	___Sometimes	___Frequently
41) Alcohol consumption	X Never	___Rarely	___Sometimes	___Frequently
42) Depression	X Never	___Rarely	___Sometimes	___Frequently
43) Shy/avoidant/withdrawn	X Never	___Rarely	___Sometimes	___Frequently
44) Suicidal threats/attempts	X Never	___Rarely	___Sometimes	___Frequently
45) Fatigued	___Never	X Rarely	___Sometimes	___Frequently
46) Anxious/nervous	___Never	X Rarely	___Sometimes	___Frequently
47) Excessive worrying	X Never	___Rarely	___Sometimes	___Frequently
48) Sleep disturbance	___Never	___Rarely	X Sometimes	___Frequently
49) Panic attacks	X Never	___Rarely	___Sometimes	___Frequently
50) Mood shifts	___Never	___Rarely	X Sometimes	___Frequently

53) For each of the behaviors noted on the previous page as occurring FREQUENTLY, or if it causes significant impairment, write a brief description of how it impacts the child's or other people's lives. Give examples. Use the back of this page as needed.

Behaviors of Concern	Impact on Child or Others
30) Fidgety/squirmy	Always moving around, constant movement, always shifting in seat.
31) Difficulty remaining seated	Can't sit still long enough in school to learn important material.
32) Runs/climbs excessively	Often climbing on furniture, runs around the house too often.
33) Difficulty playing quietly	When playing she screams, hollers, and makes unusual noises most of the time.
34) Hyperactive	Always on the go, like "climbing the walls."
35) Difficulty awaiting turn	When in line becomes fidgety, impatient, and pushy. People make comments.
36) Interrupts others	When people visit our house we can't get a word in. She won't stop at school either. Several notes sent home from teacher about this problem.
38) Poor school grades	She is intelligent, but does not take in the information because she can't sit still.

54) Briefly describe the child's ways of expressing the following emotions or behaviors:

ANGER: _____ Shouts, screams, temper tantrums when very angry. She yells, "I hate you!" _____

HAPPINESS: _Active, smiling, sometimes claps hands._

SADNESS: _____ Cries easily when sad. May slam doors for attention. _____

ANXIETY: _May stutter at times._

55) List the child's behaviors that you would like to see change: _To increase her ability to sit still and listen to other people such as teachers and family. To be able to be calm and relax._

56) Additional information you believe would be helpful: _____ None _____

PLEASE RETURN THIS AND OTHER ASSESSMENT MATERIALS TO
THIS OFFICE AT LEAST TWO DAYS BEFORE THE NEXT APPOINTMENT.

Biographical Information Form—Child

Instructions: To assist us in helping your child, please fill out this form as fully and openly as possible. All private information is held in strictest confidence within legal limits. If certain questions do not apply to the child, leave them blank.

Information supplied by: _____ Relationship:_____

Personal History

1) Child's Name: _____ 2) Age: _____ 3) Gender: __M __F

4) Weight: _____ 5) Height: _____ 6) Eye color: _____ 7) Hair color: _____ 8) Race: _____

9) Address _____
   Street & Number   City   State   Zip

10) Today's Date:_____11) Date of Birth:_____

12) Home Phone:_____13) Year in School _____

14) Has the child been involved in previous counseling?: ___ Yes ___ No
    If Yes, please describe: _____
    _____

15) Why is the child coming to counseling?:_____
    _____
    _____

16) How long has this problem persisted (from #15)?: _____

17) Under what conditions do the problems usually get worse?: _____
    _____

18) Under what conditions are the problems usually improved?:_____
    _____

Medical History

19) Name and Address of Physician(s):
    Physician's Name:_____
    Address: _____
    Street & Number   City   State   Zip
    Most Recent Physical Exam: _____ Results: _____
    _____

20) List any major illnesses and/or operations:_____
    _____
    _____

21) List any physical concerns occurring at present (e.g., high blood pressure, headaches, dizziness, etc.): _____
    _____

22) List any physical concerns (e.g., head trauma, seizures, etc.) experienced in the past:

_____

_____

23) On average how many hours of sleep does the child receive daily?: _____

24) Does the child have trouble falling asleep at night?   ___Yes ___No
   If Yes, how long has this been a problem? _____

25) Describe the child's appetite (during the past week):
   _____ poor appetite   _____ average appetite   _____ large appetite

26) What medications (and dosages) are being taken at present, and for what purpose?: _____

_____

_____

Family History

27) Mother's age:_____ If deceased, how old was the child when she passed away?: _____
28) Father's age:_____ If deceased, how old was the child when he passed away?: _____
29) If parents are separated or divorced, how old was the child then?: _____
30) Number of brother(s) _____ Their ages   _____ _____ _____ _____ _____ _____
31) Number of sister(s) _____ Their ages   _____ _____ _____ _____ _____ _____
32) Child number _____ being in a family of _____ children.
33) Is the child adopted or raised with parents other than biological parents?:   ___ Yes ___ No
34) Briefly describe the child's relationship with brothers and/or sisters:
   Biological siblings: _____

_____

_____

   Step and/or half siblings: _____

_____

_____

   Other: _____

_____

_____

35) What is the family relationship between the child and his/her custodial parents?
   Check all that apply:
   ____ Single parent mother   ____ Single parent father   _____ Parents unmarried
   ____ Parents married, together   ____ Parents divorced   _____ Parents separated
   ____ With mother and stepfather ____ With father and stepmother
   ____ Child adopted   ____ Other, describe _____

36) Is there a history or recent occurrence(s) of child abuse to this child?   ____ Yes ____ No
   If Yes, which type(s) of abuse?   ____ Verbal _____ Physical _____ Sexual
   Comments: _____

_____

2.37

37) Parents' occupations: Mother _____   Father _____

38) Briefly describe the style of parenting used in the household: _____

_____

_____

_____

_____

_____

Developmental History

39) Briefly describe any problems in the child's mother's pregnancy and/or childbirth:

_____

_____

_____

40) Please fill in when the following developmental milestones took place:

Behavior	Age began	Comments
Walking	_____	_____
Talking	_____	_____
Toilet trained	_____	_____

41) List any drugs used by mother or father at time of conception, or by mother during pregnancy:

_____

_____

42) Please rate your opinion of the child's development (compared to others the same age) in the following areas:

	Below Average	About Average	Above Average
Social	_____	_____	_____
Physical	_____	_____	_____
Language	_____	_____	_____
Intellectual	_____	_____	_____
Emotional	_____	_____	_____

For each type of development that you rated above as *below* average, please describe current areas of concern. Be specific.

_____

_____

_____

_____

_____

_____

_____

_____

43) List the child's three greatest strengths:

1) _____
2) _____
3) _____

44) List the child's three greatest weaknesses or needed areas of improvement:

1) _____
2) _____
3) _____

45) List the child's main difficulties at school:

1) _____
2) _____
3) _____

46) List the child's main difficulties at home:

1) _____
2) _____
3) _____

47) Briefly describe the child's friendships: _____
_____
_____

48) What report card grades does the child usually receive?: _____
Have these changed lately?: ___ Yes ___ No If Yes, how?:_____

49) Briefly describe the child's hobbies and interests: _____
_____

50) Describe how the child is disciplined: _____
_____
_____
_____

51) For what reasons is the child disciplined? _____
_____
_____

Behaviors of Concern

52) Please check how often the following behaviors occur. Those occurring FREQUENTLY or of special concern may be described on the next page.

Behavior				
1) Loses temper easily	___Never	___Rarely	___Sometimes	___Frequently
2) Argues with adults	___Never	___Rarely	___Sometimes	___Frequently
3) Refuses adults' requests	___Never	___Rarely	___Sometimes	___Frequently
4) Deliberately annoys people	___Never	___Rarely	___Sometimes	___Frequently
5) Blames others for own mistakes	___Never	___Rarely	___Sometimes	___Frequently
6) Easily annoyed by others	___Never	___Rarely	___Sometimes	___Frequently
7) Angry/resentful	___Never	___Rarely	___Sometimes	___Frequently
8) Spiteful/vindictive	___Never	___Rarely	___Sometimes	___Frequently
9) Defiant	___Never	___Rarely	___Sometimes	___Frequently
10) Bullies/teases others	___Never	___Rarely	___Sometimes	___Frequently
11) Initiates fights	___Never	___Rarely	___Sometimes	___Frequently
12) Uses a weapon	___Never	___Rarely	___Sometimes	___Frequently
13) Physically cruel to people	___Never	___Rarely	___Sometimes	___Frequently
14) Physically cruel to animals	___Never	___Rarely	___Sometimes	___Frequently
15) Stealing	___Never	___Rarely	___Sometimes	___Frequently
16) Forced sexual activity	___Never	___Rarely	___Sometimes	___Frequently
17) Intentional arson	___Never	___Rarely	___Sometimes	___Frequently
18) Burglary	___Never	___Rarely	___Sometimes	___Frequently
19) "Cons" other people	___Never	___Rarely	___Sometimes	___Frequently
20) Runs away from home	___Never	___Rarely	___Sometimes	___Frequently
21) Truant at school	___Never	___Rarely	___Sometimes	___Frequently
22) Doesn't pay attention to details	___Never	___Rarely	___Sometimes	___Frequently
23) Several careless mistakes	___Never	___Rarely	___Sometimes	___Frequently
24) Does not listen when spoken to	___Never	___Rarely	___Sometimes	___Frequently
25) Doesn't finish chores/homework	___Never	___Rarely	___Sometimes	___Frequently
26) Difficulty organizing tasks	___Never	___Rarely	___Sometimes	___Frequently
27) Loses things	___Never	___Rarely	___Sometimes	___Frequently
28) Easily distracted	___Never	___Rarely	___Sometimes	___Frequently
29) Forgetful in daily activities	___Never	___Rarely	___Sometimes	___Frequently
30) Fidgety/squirmy	___Never	___Rarely	___Sometimes	___Frequently
31) Difficulty remaining seated	___Never	___Rarely	___Sometimes	___Frequently
32) Runs/climbs around excessively	___Never	___Rarely	___Sometimes	___Frequently
33) Difficulty playing quietly	___Never	___Rarely	___Sometimes	___Frequently
34) Hyperactive	___Never	___Rarely	___Sometimes	___Frequently
35) Difficulty awaiting turn	___Never	___Rarely	___Sometimes	___Frequently
36) Interrupts others	___Never	___Rarely	___Sometimes	___Frequently
37) Problems pronouncing words	___Never	___Rarely	___Sometimes	___Frequently
38) Poor grades in school	___Never	___Rarely	___Sometimes	___Frequently
39) Expelled from school	___Never	___Rarely	___Sometimes	___Frequently
40) Drug abuse	___Never	___Rarely	___Sometimes	___Frequently
41) Alcohol consumption	___Never	___Rarely	___Sometimes	___Frequently
42) Depression	___Never	___Rarely	___Sometimes	___Frequently
43) Shy/avoidant/withdrawn	___Never	___Rarely	___Sometimes	___Frequently
44) Suicidal threats/attempts	___Never	___Rarely	___Sometimes	___Frequently
45) Fatigued	___Never	___Rarely	___Sometimes	___Frequently
46) Anxious/nervous	___Never	___Rarely	___Sometimes	___Frequently
47) Excessive worrying	___Never	___Rarely	___Sometimes	___Frequently
48) Sleep disturbance	___Never	___Rarely	___Sometimes	___Frequently
49) Panic attacks	___Never	___Rarely	___Sometimes	___Frequently
50) Mood shifts	___Never	___Rarely	___Sometimes	___Frequently

53) For each of the behaviors noted on the previous page as occurring FREQUENTLY, or if it causes significant impairment, write a brief description of how it impacts the child's or other people's lives. Give examples. Use the back of this page as needed.

Behaviors of Concern   Impact on Child or Others

_____   _____
_____   _____
_____   _____
_____   _____
_____   _____
_____   _____
_____   _____
_____   _____
_____   _____
_____   _____
_____   _____
_____   _____

54) Briefly describe the child's ways of expressing the following emotions or behaviors:
ANGER: _____
HAPPINESS: _____
SADNESS: _____
ANXIETY: _____

55) List the child's behaviors that you would like to see change: _____
_____
_____
_____
_____
_____

56) Additional information you believe would be helpful: _____
_____
_____
_____
_____
_____
_____

PLEASE RETURN THIS AND OTHER ASSESSMENT MATERIALS TO
THIS OFFICE AT LEAST TWO DAYS BEFORE THE NEXT APPOINTMENT.

Emotional/
Behavioral
Assessment

The form starting on page 2.43 is primarily used for children and people diagnosed with developmental disabilities. It is designed to solicit information about the client's current level of emotional expression, positive behaviors, behaviors targeted for change, and recent stressors. It further helps set treatment plan goals.

Emotional/Behavioral Assessment

Name _Christine Watters_   Date _4-6-97_
         (answers apply to)   DOB _3-6-91_   Age _6-1_
Residence ___(family residence)___   Phone _555-8899_
Address ___45678 Hayward St.___
         ___Tacoma, WA 99889___
Respondent's Name ___Lisa Watters___   Relationship ___Mother___

Please Use the Back of Any Sheet if More Space Is Needed

1) Check the following behaviors or skills that describe positive characteristics of the client. (Add others that apply.)

X Accepts praise	__ Friendly	__ Polite
X Affectionate	__ Gregarious	__ Reading/writing
__ Apologizes	X Grooming/hygiene	__ Respects others
X Assertive	__ Helpful	__ Responsible
__ Cleanliness (household)	X Hobbies/crafts	__ Safety skills
X Community skills	__ Honesty	X Sense of humor
__ Cooperative	X Independent	__ Shares
X Courteous	__ Insightful	__ Survival skills
X Daily living skills	__ Listening skills	__ Verbal expression
__ Dependable	__ Money management skills	__ Works hard
__ Emotional expression	__ Motivated	__ _____
__ Eye contact	__ Organized	__ _____
__ _____	__ _____	__ _____

Comments on any of the above: _She is a good girl, but just can't stay with any one activity_
for very long. She tries to be helpful, but goes on to something else.

2) Which of the following normal emotions or responses do you recognize as at least sometimes taking place with the client? (Add others that apply.)

X Anger	X Embarrassment	__ Grief
X Anxiety	__ Envy	X Happiness
X Boredom	__ Fear	__ Loneliness
__ Depression	X Frustration	X Stress
__ _____	__ _____	__ _____

3) List any concerns you have regarding any of the above emotions or responses.
She gets angry and frustrated too easily. This makes her more hyperactive.

4) How does s/he express (verbally and nonverbally) the following emotions?

HAPPINESS _When Christine is happy she is much more helpful around the house. She smiles and might sing. She doesn't directly say she is happy._

SADNESS _She initially will be mopey and withdrawn. After a while she might act like she is mad at everybody. She cries very easily, but doesn't seem to recognize depression._

ANGER _Temper tantrums. It doesn't take much for her to hit people or throw things in her room. At times she will verbally abuse others._

FRUSTRATION _Same as anger._

5) Briefly describe any self-injurious behaviors (SIBs) and/or inappropriate self-stimulation behaviors (SSBs).

Behavior (describe the problem behavior)
Antecedents (describe what usually takes place before the behavior occurs)
Consequences (describe what actions are taken after the behavior occurs)
Frequency/duration (describe how often and for how long it occurs)

Behavior _None_
Antecedents _____
Consequences _____
Frequency/duration _____

Behavior _____
Antecedents _____
Consequences _____
Frequency/duration _____

Behavior _____
Antecedents _____
Consequences _____
Frequency/duration _____

6) Briefly describe aggressive acts (to people or property).

Behavior _____ _Temper tantrums_
Antecedents _____ _When she does not get her way_
Consequences _____ _Time out in her room, lose upcoming privileges_
Frequency/duration _____ _4–5 times per week/15–30 minutes_

Behavior _____ _Inappropriate yelling at family members_
Antecedents _____ _When she is frustrated or not able to get things immediately_
Consequences _____ _Time out, lose privileges_
Frequency/duration _____ _3–4 times per week/varies_

Behavior _____ _Throw toys against wall_
Antecedents _____ _When she is mad at her sister_
Consequences _____ _Must apologize, time out_
Frequency/duration _____ _1 time per week_

7) Describe any inappropriate sexual behavior. ✗None known

_____
_____
_____

8) Describe any inappropriate social behaviors. __None known
Children at school tease her because of her hyperactivity and immaturity. She then acts
even more immature and may cry and receive more teasing. She is beginning to lash out
physically at her classmates.

9) How would you rate his/her listening skills?

Low		Average		High	__NA
1	②	3	4	5	

Comments _____ _She hears but rarely listens. She is too active to have time for listening._

10) How would you rate his/her ability to cope with problems?

Low		Average		High	__NA
①	2	3	4	5	

Comments _____ _Very poor_

11) How would you rate his/her respect for other people?

Low		Average		High	__NA
1	*②*	3	4	5	

Comments _____

12) How would you rate his/her ability to manage anger?

Low		Average		High	__NA
①	2	3	4	5	

Comments _____

13) How would you rate his/her motivation to change negative behaviors?

Low		Average		High	__NA
1	*②*	3	4	5	

Comments _____

14) How would you rate his/her ability to accept constructive criticism?

Low		Average		High	__NA
1	2	*③*	4	5	

Comments _____

15) How would you rate his/her potential for increased independent living?

Low		Average		High	__NA
1	2	*③*	4	5	

Comments _____

16) Please list any significant stressful events or major changes in his/her life in the past six months (e.g., loss of loved ones, significant others moving, change in residence, new roommate or housemate, new sibling, major illness, etc.).   __None known

Her grandmother died about four months ago. _____

_____

_____

_____

If applicable, what behavioral/emotional effects may this have had?   __None known

She spent every Saturday at her grandmother's home. They were very close. Although
Christine was hyperactive before her grandmother died, she has been much more defiant
in the past few months.

_____

17) Check any of the following which apply to him/her. (Add others that apply.)

__Anxiety	X Explosive behaviors	__Schizophrenia
__Auditory hallucinations	X Impulse control concerns	__Sexual concerns
__Chemical dependency	__Mood shifts	__Social withdrawal
X Conduct problems	__Obsessive/compulsive	__Suicidal threats
__Depression	__Paranoid	__Thought disorder
__Eating disorder	__Phobias/fears	__Visual hallucinations
__ _____	__ _____	__ _____

Describe behavioral effects or incidents of each of the above items.

Conduct problems and explosive behaviors: When she does not get her way she gets very frustrated and, at times, will lash out at anything or anyone in her way. It does not take much to set her off. She has never hurt anyone. She usually has a tantrum, then cools off after about ½ hour, especially if she gets no attention for the tantrum.

Impulse control: She can't wait for anything. She often gets into trouble at school for cutting in line. She always wants things before it is the right time. She gets edgy when she has to wait.

18) Briefly describe any past events that may be difficult for him/her to handle at this time (e.g., abuse, injuries).

None known.

19) Briefly describe any past events that were particularly encouraging or led to positive life changes for him/her.

20) Please list any other information about him/her (e.g., important background information, special strengths/weaknesses, concerns with other people, problems on the job, etc.)

Emotional/Behavioral Assessment

Name _____   Date _____
         (answers apply to)   DOB _____ Age _____

Residence _____   Phone _____

Address _____

_____

Respondent's Name _____   Relationship _____

Please Use the Back of Any Sheet if More Space Is Needed

1) Check the following behaviors or skills that describe positive characteristics of the client. (Add others that apply.)

__Accepts praise	__Friendly	__Polite
__Affectionate	__Gregarious	__Reading/writing
__Apologizes	__Grooming/hygiene	__Respects others
__Assertive	__Helpful	__Responsible
__Cleanliness (household)	__Hobbies/crafts	__Safety skills
__Community skills	__Honesty	__Sense of humor
__Cooperative	__Independent	__Shares
__Courteous	__Insightful	__Survival skills
__Daily living skills	__Listening skills	__Verbal expression
__Dependable	__Money management skills	__Works hard
__Emotional expression	__Motivated	__ _____
__Eye contact	__Organized	__ _____
__ _____	__ _____	__ _____

Comments on any of the above: _____

_____

2) Which of the following normal emotions or responses do you recognize as at least sometimes taking place with the client? (Add others that apply.)

__Anger	__Embarrassment	__Grief
__Anxiety	__Envy	__Happiness
__Boredom	__Fear	__Loneliness
__Depression	__Frustration	__Stress
__ _____	__ _____	__ _____

3) List any concerns you have regarding any of the above emotions or responses.

_____

_____

4) How does s/he express (verbally and nonverbally) the following emotions?

HAPPINESS _____
_____
_____

SADNESS _____
_____
_____

ANGER _____
_____
_____

FRUSTRATION _____
_____
_____

5) Briefly describe any self-injurious behaviors (SIBs) and/or inappropriate self-stimulation behaviors (SSBs).

Behavior (describe the problem behavior)
Antecedents (describe what usually takes place before the behavior occurs)
Consequences (describe what actions are taken after the behavior occurs)
Frequency/duration (describe how often and for how long it occurs)

Behavior _____
Antecedents _____
Consequences _____
Frequency/duration _____

Behavior _____
Antecedents _____
Consequences _____
Frequency/duration _____

Behavior _____
Antecedents _____
Consequences _____
Frequency/duration _____

6) Briefly describe aggressive acts (to people or property).

Behavior _____

Antecedents _____

Consequences _____

Frequency/duration _____

Behavior _____

Antecedents _____

Consequences _____

Frequency/duration _____

Behavior _____

Antecedents _____

Consequences _____

Frequency/duration _____

7) Describe any inappropriate sexual behavior.   __None known

_____

_____

_____

8) Describe any inappropriate social behaviors.   __None known

_____

_____

_____

9) How would you rate his/her listening skills?

Low		Average		High	__NA
1	2	3	4	5	

Comments _____

10) How would you rate his/her ability to cope with problems?

Low		Average		High	__NA
1	2	3	4	5	

Comments _____

11) How would you rate his/her respect for other people?

Low		Average		High	__NA
1	2	3	4	5	

Comments _____

12) How would you rate his/her ability to manage anger?

Low		Average		High	__NA
1	2	3	4	5	

Comments _____

13) How would you rate his/her motivation to change negative behaviors?

Low		Average		High	__NA
1	2	3	4	5	

Comments _____

14) How would you rate his/her ability to accept constructive criticism?

Low		Average		High	__NA
1	2	3	4	5	

Comments _____

15) How would you rate his/her potential for increased independent living?

Low		Average		High	__NA
1	2	3	4	5	

Comments _____

16) Please list any significant stressful events or major changes in his/her life in the past six months (e.g., loss of loved ones, significant others moving, change in residence, new roommate or housemate, new sibling, major illness, etc.) __None known

_____

_____

_____

_____

If applicable, what behavioral/emotional effects may this have had? __None known

_____

_____

_____

_____

17) Check any of the following which apply to him/her. (Add others that apply.)

__Anxiety	__Explosive behaviors	__Schizophrenia
__Auditory hallucinations	__Impulse control concerns	__Sexual concerns
__Chemical dependency	__Mood shifts	__Social withdrawal
__Conduct problems	__Obsessive/compulsive	__Suicidal threats
__Depression	__Paranoid	__Thought disorder
__Eating disorder	__Phobias/fears	__Visual hallucinations
__ _____	__ _____	__ _____

Describe behavioral effects or incidents of each of the above items.

_____

_____

_____

_____

_____

_____

_____

18) Briefly describe any past events that may be difficult for him/her to handle at this time (e.g., abuse, injuries).

_____

_____

_____

19) Briefly describe any past events that were particularly encouraging or led to positive life changes for him/her.

_____

_____

_____

20) Please list any other information about him/her (e.g., important background information, special strengths/weaknesses, concerns with other people, problems on the job, etc.)

_____

_____

_____

_____

_____

_____

_____

Diagnostic Assessment Report

The Diagnostic Assessment Report (see page 2.54) is designed to summarize the intake and assessment material, providing clear documentation of the client's current mental health condition—presenting problem, history, current functional impairments, and mental status. The report includes specific examples of frequency, duration, and intensity of symptoms.

In the Diagnosis Validation section of the form, the therapist may use diagnostic material such as testing, biographical data, collateral information, and intake material to document the diagnosis. This section may be especially helpful for an audit, for forensics, and in justifying the need for further services.

This form has proved useful in at least two ways. First, it helps the therapist to keep on target in documenting the diagnosis and treatment. Second, it has been found helpful to send this form in to third-party payers along with their request form for additional service authorization.

Judy Doe

The Diagnosis Validation form for Judy Doe provides clear validation of supporting material for a diagnosis of major depression. Information provided in the form is a summary of the previous assessment material.

Diagnostic Assessment Report

Name _____ *Judy Doe* _____   Therapist _____ *DLB* _____

Intake/Assessment Date(s) _____ *3-8-97 & 3-15-97* _____   Report Date _____ *3-16-97* _____

1) Purpose of Visit/Current Life Situation (Include duration/frequency of symptoms)
Self-referred. Has felt increasingly more sad for past year (average 3 of 4 days). Usually fatigued. Increased withdrawal has led to loss of two friends (with whom she used to be close) in past month. Now avoids them. Spouse threatening to leave soon due to her anger outbursts and lack of sexual activity. Describes marriage as "on the rocks." May desire marital counseling at a later date. Quite dissatisfied with teaching career, home life, and self. Little/no motivation to "get things done." Misses 2–4 days of work per month in past year due to "boredom/frustration with job." Currently finds no pleasures in life.

2) History of Current Problem/Developmental Incidents/Treatment History/Medications, etc.
Prior counseling for depression in 1967–1968 due to depression after breaking up with a college boyfriend. Does not remember the focus of the sessions, but believes that depression was alleviated until approximately the past year or so. Now feeling "depressed, like when in college." No meds at that time. Increased marital conflict developing, little time spent together; generally shouting, blaming, no sex or intimacy. Markedly decreased satisfaction as schoolteacher. Several self-deprecating statements regarding teaching and parenting effectiveness. Past two years insomnia. Wakes up 3–4x/night. No mania. Past year lost 20#. Views life as "monotonous, uneventful, boring." Exercises 3x/week, but not fun. Wants to "start feeling human again."

3) Current Functioning, Symptoms, and Impairments (e.g., occupational, social, emotional)
1) Impaired social functioning (previously spent 1–2 evenings per week with friends, now is rarely with others). Has lost friends, initiates little/no social interactions. 2) Marital conflict leading to increased anxiety level. Avoiding family/friends. 3) Occupational impairment; missing 2–4 days/month (1 year ago rarely missed work), views teaching performance as poor at this time. 4) Emotional impairment; sad most of time, fatigued, anhedonia, low ego strength.

STRENGTHS _____ *Moderately motivated to change. Religious reasons vs. suicidality.*

WEAKNESSES _____ *Seems to blame others for past failures. Level of insight.*

4) Family Mental Health History *Describes family of origin as functional. 2nd of 5 children. Left home at age 18 (college). No known family Hx of depression or other mental health concerns. Historically good communication with family. Hx of mother and older sibling helping/making several of her decisions. Family generally provides positive social support, but often viewed as intrusive by client.*

5) Other (Substance abuse, suicidal ideations, court referral, etc.) *Does not view self as chemically dependent. No suicidal plan; ideations when stressed. Signed Limits of Confidentiality. Contracted for actions to be taken when experiencing suicidal thoughts: given phone numbers for Therapist, Crisis Hotline, and Mental Health Intake.*

Mental Status Exam

		Normal 0	Slight 1	2	Moderate 3	4	5	Severe 6
APPEARANCE	Unkempt, unclean, disheveled	O	O	O	●	O	O	O
	Clothing and/or grooming atypical	●	O	O	O	O	O	O
	Unusual physical characteristics	●	O	O	O	O	O	O

Comments re: Appearance *T-shirt and jogging pants, moderately groomed, hair somewhat dishevelled.*

		Normal 0	Slight 1	2	Moderate 3	4	5	Severe 6
POSTURE	Slumped	O	O	O	O	●	O	O
	Rigid, tense	O	O	●	O	O	O	O
FACIAL EXPRESSIONS SUGGEST	Anxiety	O	●	O	O	O	O	O
	Depression, sadness	O	O	O	O	O	●	O
	Absence of feeling, blandness	O	O	O	O	●	O	O
	Atypical, unusual	●	O	O	O	O	O	O
GENERAL BODY MOVEMENTS	Accelerated, increased speed	●	O	O	O	O	O	O
	Decreased, slowed	O	O	O	O	●	O	O
	Atypical, unusual	●	O	O	O	O	O	O
	Restless, fidgety	O	●	O	O	O	O	O
SPEECH	Rapid speech	●	O	O	O	O	O	O
	Slowed speech	O	O	O	O	●	O	O
	Loud speech	●	O	O	O	O	O	O
	Soft speech	O	O	O	●	O	O	O
	Mute	●	O	O	O	O	O	O
	Atypical quality (e.g., slurring)	O	●	O	O	O	O	O
THERAPIST/ CLIENT RELATIONSHIP	Domineering, controlling	●	O	O	O	O	O	O
	Submissive, compliant, dependent	O	O	O	O	●	O	O
	Provocative, hostile, challenging	●	O	O	O	O	O	O
	Suspicious, guarded, evasive	●	O	O	O	O	O	O
	Uncooperative, noncompliant	●	O	O	O	O	O	O

Comments re: Behavior *Low eye contact.*

		Normal 0	Slight 1	2	Moderate 3	4	5	Severe 6
AFFECT/ MOOD	Inappropriate to thought content	●	O	O	O	O	O	O
	Increased lability of affect	●	O	O	O	O	O	O
	Blunted, dulled, bland	O	O	O	●	O	O	O
	Euphoria, elation	●	O	O	O	O	O	O
	Anger, hostility	O	O	●	O	O	O	O
	Anxiety, fear, apprehension	O	●	O	O	O	O	O
	Depression, sadness	O	O	O	O	●	O	O

Comments re: Affect *Behavior, speech, and affect concordant. Onset of most recent episode of depression in past year. Depressed 3 or 4 days, most of day. Daily crying spells, cries when alone. Easily annoyed, but does not express frustration.*

		Normal	Slight		Moderate			Severe
		0	1	2	3	4	5	6
PERCEPTION	Illusions	●	O	O	O	O	O	O
	Auditory hallucinations	●	O	O	O	O	O	O
	Visual hallucinations	●	O	O	O	O	O	O
	Other hallucinations	●	O	O	O	O	O	O

Comments re: Perception _None_

		Normal	Slight		Moderate			Severe
INTELLECTUAL	Level of consciousness	●	O	O	O	O	O	O
FUNCTIONING	Attention span, distractible	O	O	●	O	O	O	O
IMPAIRMENTS	Abstract thinking	●	O	O	O	O	O	O
	Calculation ability	●	O	O	O	O	O	O
	Intelligence	●	O	O	O	O	O	O
ORIENTATION	Time	●	O	O	O	O	O	O
	Place	●	O	O	O	O	O	O
	Person	●	O	O	O	O	O	O
MEMORY	Recent	O	●	O	O	O	O	O
IMPAIRMENT	Remote	●	O	O	O	O	O	O
INSIGHT	Denies psych problems	O	O	●	O	O	O	O
	Blames others	O	●	O	O	O	O	O
JUDGMENT	Decision making	O	O	O	●	O	O	O
IMPAIRMENTS	Impulse control	O	O	O	O	●	O	O
THOUGHT	Obsessions	●	O	O	O	O	O	O
CONTENT	Compulsions	●	O	O	O	O	O	O
	Phobias	●	O	O	O	O	O	O
	Depersonalization	●	O	O	O	O	O	O
	Suicial ideation	O	O	O	●	O	O	O
	Homicidal ideation	●	O	O	O	O	O	O
	Delusions	●	O	O	O	O	O	O

Comments re: Thinking _Historical incidents of poor judgment and impulsivity with subsequent depression. At times will withdraw or miss work when frustrated. Denies suicidal attempts. Ideations at times. Blames self for not motivating spouse, children, and students._

Diagnosis Validation

PRIMARY DIAGNOSIS _296.32 Major depression, recurrent, moderate, w/o psychotic features_

NAME OF TEST
Minnesota Multiphasic
Personality Inventory—2
(MMPI-2)
Beck Depression
Inventory (BDI)

RESULTS
Elevated 2-4-7 Depression, anxiety, CD potential
Profile typical of cycles of acting out, guilt, depression
Raw score 32—Severe

Biographical Information (Specific BIF references) _Frequent feelings of_
hopelessness, loneliness, no one caring, failure, disappointment, can't do anything right,
difficulties concentrating, depression, and having no emotions. Unwanted Sx of avoiding
people, depression, fatigue, hopelessness, loneliness, loss of sexual interest, frequent sickness,
sleeping difficulties, suicidal thoughts, withdrawal, and worrying. Experiences little/no
pleasure.

Collateral Information
Have requested records from previous therapist.

Case/Intake Notes, MSE References (Include brief descriptions, dates, and line numbers)
3-8-97, Intake Notes. Section 8: poor appetite; 13: Crying spells daily, fatigued, low
ego strength, social withdrawal increasing; 14: psychomotor retardation, blunted affect,
difficulty making decisions, suicidal ideation, appeared depressed; 15: usually feels depressed,
guilt feelings, insomnia.

2.57

DIAGNOSIS 2 _Deferred_ _____ (Make copies for additional Dx's)

NAME OF TEST   **RESULTS**

_____   _____

_____   _____

Biographical Information (Specific BIF references) _____

_____

_____

_____

_____

Case/Intake Notes, MSE References, Collateral (Include brief descriptions, dates and line numbers)

_____

_____

_____

_____

_____

_____

_____

DIAGNOSTIC IMPRESSIONS

Axis I   _296.32 Major depression, recurrent, moderate, w/o psychotic features_

Axis II   _Deferred_

Axis III   _Defer to physician_

Axis IV   _Spousal discord, loss of friends_

Axis V   _Global Assessment of Functioning (GAF): Current: 58_   _Past year: 78_

Needed Mental Health Services

____ Further assessment (specify) _____

_X_ Individual   ___Group   ___Family   ___Other (specify) _____

Other Needed Services

_X_ Psychiatric consultation   _X_ Physical exam   ___Neurological consultation

____ CD evaluation   ____ Other (specify) _____

Did client/guardian sign the treatment plan? _X_Yes ___No

Was Dx explained to client? _X_Yes ___No

Darlene L. Benton, Ph.D. _____   ____ _3-16-97_ ____

Therapist's Signature   Date

Sharon Bell, Ph.D. _____   ____ _3-16-97_ ____

Supervisor's Signature   Date

Diagnostic Assessment Report

Name _____   Therapist _____

Intake/Assessment Date(s)   _____   Report Date _____

1) Purpose of Visit/Current Life Situation (Include duration/frequency of symptoms)

_____

_____

_____

_____

_____

2) History of Current Problem/Developmental Incidents/Treatment History/Medications, etc.

_____

_____

_____

_____

_____

_____

_____

3) Current Functioning, Symptoms, and Impairments (e.g., occupational, social, emotional)

_____

_____

_____

_____

STRENGTHS _____

WEAKNESSES _____

4) Family Mental Health History _____

_____

_____

_____

5) Other (Substance abuse, suicidal ideations, court referral, etc.) _____

_____

_____

_____

Mental Status Exam

		Normal 0	Slight 1	2	Moderate 3	4	5	Severe 6
APPEARANCE	Unkempt, unclean, disheveled	O	O	O	O	O	O	O
	Clothing and/or grooming atypical	O	O	O	O	O	O	O
	Unusual physical characteristics	O	O	O	O	O	O	O

Comments re: Appearance _____

_____

		Normal 0	Slight 1	2	Moderate 3	4	5	Severe 6
POSTURE	Slumped	O	O	O	O	O	O	O
	Rigid, tense	O	O	O	O	O	O	O
FACIAL EXPRESSIONS SUGGEST	Anxiety	O	O	O	O	O	O	O
	Depression, sadness	O	O	O	O	O	O	O
	Absence of feeling, blandness	O	O	O	O	O	O	O
	Atypical, unusual	O	O	O	O	O	O	O
GENERAL BODY MOVEMENTS	Accelerated, increased speed	O	O	O	O	O	O	O
	Decreased, slowed	O	O	O	O	O	O	O
	Atypical, unusual	O	O	O	O	O	O	O
	Restless, fidgety	O	O	O	O	O	O	O
SPEECH	Rapid speech	O	O	O	O	O	O	O
	Slowed speech	O	O	O	O	O	O	O
	Loud speech	O	O	O	O	O	O	O
	Soft speech	O	O	O	O	O	O	O
	Mute	O	O	O	O	O	O	O
	Atypical quality (e.g., slurring)	O	O	O	O	O	O	O
THERAPIST/ CLIENT RELATIONSHIP	Domineering, controlling	O	O	O	O	O	O	O
	Submissive, compliant, dependent	O	O	O	O	O	O	O
	Provocative, hostile, challenging	O	O	O	O	O	O	O
	Suspicious, guarded, evasive	O	O	O	O	O	O	O
	Uncooperative, noncompliant	O	O	O	O	O	O	O

Comments re: Behavior_____

_____

		Normal 0	Slight 1	2	Moderate 3	4	5	Severe 6
AFFECT/ MOOD	Inappropriate to thought content	O	O	O	O	O	O	O
	Increased lability of affect	O	O	O	O	O	O	O
	Blunted, dulled, bland	O	O	O	O	O	O	O
	Euphoria, elation	O	O	O	O	O	O	O
	Anger, hostility	O	O	O	O	O	O	O
	Anxiety, fear, apprehension	O	O	O	O	O	O	O
	Depression, sadness	O	O	O	O	O	O	O

Comments re: Affect_____

_____

		Normal	Slight		Moderate			Severe
		0	1	2	3	4	5	6
PERCEPTION	Illusions	O	O	O	O	O	O	O
	Auditory hallucinations	O	O	O	O	O	O	O
	Visual hallucinations	O	O	O	O	O	O	O
	Other hallucinations	O	O	O	O	O	O	O

Comments re: Perception _____

_____

		Normal	Slight		Moderate			Severe
INTELLECTUAL	Level of consciousness	O	O	O	O	O	O	O
FUNCTIONING	Attention span, distractible	O	O	O	O	O	O	O
IMPAIRMENTS	Abstract thinking	O	O	O	O	O	O	O
	Calculation ability	O	O	O	O	O	O	O
	Intelligence	O	O	O	O	O	O	O
ORIENTATION	Time	O	O	O	O	O	O	O
	Place	O	O	O	O	O	O	O
	Person	O	O	O	O	O	O	O
MEMORY	Recent	O	O	O	O	O	O	O
IMPAIRMENT	Remote	O	O	O	O	O	O	O
INSIGHT	Denies psych problems	O	O	O	O	O	O	O
	Blames others	O	O	O	O	O	O	O
JUDGMENT	Decision making	O	O	O	O	O	O	O
IMPAIRMENTS	Impulse control	O	O	O	O	O	O	O
THOUGHT	Obsessions	O	O	O	O	O	O	O
CONTENT	Compulsions	O	O	O	O	O	O	O
	Phobias	O	O	O	O	O	O	O
	Depersonalization	O	O	O	O	O	O	O
	Suicial ideation	O	O	O	O	O	O	O
	Homicidal ideation	O	O	O	O	O	O	O
	Delusions	O	O	O	O	O	O	O

Comments re: Thinking _____

_____
_____
_____

Diagnosis Validation

PRIMARY DIAGNOSIS _____

NAME OF TEST   **RESULTS**

_____   _____
_____   _____
_____   _____
_____   _____
_____   _____

Biographical Information (Specific BIF references) _____

_____
_____
_____
_____
_____
_____
_____

Collateral Information

_____
_____
_____
_____
_____

Case/Intake Notes, MSE References (Include brief descriptions, dates, and line numbers)

_____
_____
_____
_____
_____
_____
_____
_____
_____
_____
_____

DIAGNOSIS 2 _____   (make copies for
                                                             additional Dx's)

NAME OF TEST   **RESULTS**

_____   _____

_____   _____

Biographical Information (Specific BIF references) _____

_____

_____

_____

_____

Case/Intake Notes, MSE References, Collateral (Include brief descriptions, dates and line numbers)

_____

_____

_____

_____

_____

_____

_____

DIAGNOSTIC IMPRESSIONS

Axis I   _____

              _____

Axis II   _____

              _____

Axis III   _____

Axis IV   _____

Axis V   _____

Needed Mental Health Services

___ Further assessment (specify) _____

___ Individual   ___Group   ___Family   ___Other (specify) _____

Other Needed Services

___ Psychiatric consultation   ___ Physical exam   ___Neurological consultation

___ CD evaluation   ___ Other (specify) _____

Did client/guardian sign the treatment plan?   __Yes   __No

Was Dx explained to client?   __Yes   __No

_____   _____

Therapist's Signature   Date

_____   _____

Supervisor's Signature   Date

Chapter 3

Evaluation Forms
and Procedures

Generally much more information is needed when a psychological evaluation has been requested, compared to the information required for a client entering a few sessions of therapy. But the following psychological evaluation forms may also be used prior to therapy when needed.

Although the examples of psychological evaluation forms for adults (page 3.4) and children (page 3.28) are similar, several differences exist, such as the use of collateral information provided by parents, developmental issues, diagnostic categories, and the Mental Status Exam. Each may be used for general purposes and formal evaluations such as Social Security Disability evaluations. A structured interview format is employed from which the final report may be easily dictated. A sample of both an adult and child evaluation are included.

Adult and Child Psychological Evaluations

The psychological evaluation is a structured interview designed to provide symptoms, history, daily activities, ability to relate to others, substance abuse, and an extensive mental status evaluation. The form is also designed to help evaluate thought, affective, personality, and somatoform disorders, plus memory and concentration.

These forms are not ends in themselves; rather, they provide structure for an interview and subsequent data for a psychological report or treatment plan. The requested information in each section is self-explanatory for those trained in diagnostic interviewing and mental status evaluations.

Adult Psychological Evaluation

Client's Name _George Wallington_   Date _4-8-97_

SSN _999-99-9999_   DOB _3-7-55_

Allegations (Presenting problem) _Anxiety, memory/concentration problems_

Collateral information by _Martha Wallington_   Relationship _Spouse_

Other Information _Driven to appointment by spouse_

A. PHYSICAL DESCRIPTION

Identification given _State driver's license_   Gender _M_   Age _42_

Race _Caucasian_   Height _5-11_   Weight _195_   Eyes _Brown_   Hair _Brown_

Other descriptors of appearance _Tattoo on right forearm_

B. HISTORY

1) Signs and symptoms

Purpose of evaluation. Specific concerns and functional impairments (e.g., social, occupational, affective, cognitive, memory, physical, etc.).

Feeling anxious and having trouble concentrating since auto accident. Lost job of 12 years' duration as programmer. (Could not concentrate, missed much work due to anxiety, not performing work functions adequately.) Has tried less demanding jobs, but too easily confused. Difficulties coping with new situations. Increasing social anxiety.

Impacts of impairments on functioning _Has tried driving, but got lost when drove on road not previously known. Social anxiety increasing, emergent withdrawal and isolation. Begins household chores, but forgets in middle of task._

As seen by professional _Appeared confused and anxious. Asked to have several questions repeated. Some stuttering and word finding._

2) History of present illness

Onset of impairment _Auto accident 3-8-96. Closed head injury left side. Anxiety level has increased over past 2–3 months._

Previous diagnoses (by whom?) _No previous mental health diagnosis. Records indicate closed head injury (left side)._

Course of illness   __ Improving   __ Stable   _X_ Deteriorating

Client's spouse notes physical and speech improvements since accident, but over past few months several concerns in levels of anxiety and confusion. Forgetting simple requests that were not a concern in the past (short shopping lists, people's names, tasks begun, words). Past few months does not want to leave house/property due to panic symptoms.

Events affecting frequency and duration *New situations, especially those which are challenging* *or somewhat stressful, increase anxiety and confusion. Much anxiety in crowds of people* *whom he does not know or when in unfamiliar places.*

Precipitating factors (emotional, environmental, social) *Cognitive challenges and almost* *anything unfamiliar.*

Previous/current mental health treatment (and its effectiveness) *No Hx or current mental* *health Tx.*

Current/previous medications *Meds for seizures, did not know name of med.*

Compliance? _____ X _____   Effectiveness *No seizures since accident*

Hospitalizations/treatment *After accident was in coma 1 week, subsequently hospitalized 2* *months.*

Current special services (social, educational, legal) *Speech and physical therapy 2x/week.*

NOTE AND RESOLVE ANY DISCREPANCIES BETWEEN INFORMATION GIVEN AND WHAT RECORDS INDICATE. *None noted.*

BEGIN 5/30-MINUTE MEMORY CHECK *Memorize car/jump/pencil*

Activities of Daily Living
C. CURRENT LEVEL OF DAILY FUNCTIONING
1) Current hobbies, interests, and scope of interests

Hobby/interest

How persistently is it followed?

	Frequency	Duration
Fishing	*1 x/week*	*2–3 hrs.*
Yard work	*daily*	*1–2 hrs.*
Crossword puzzles (as per M.D.)	*daily*	*½ hr.*

Realistic, appropriate, compare to previous functioning *Realistic during time of recovery,* *but significantly reduced level of cognitive functioning compared to previous functioning.*

3.5

2) Activities

Do you live in a ___X house ___ apartment ___ townhouse ___ condo ___ mobile home

Who else lives there? (relationships, ages) _Spouse, 2 daughters (4, 12), 1 son (10)_

_____

What kinds of things do you usually eat for

Breakfast _Cereal, toast_

Lunch ___Sandwich_

Dinner ___Heat up microwave food_

Do you have physical problems in bathing/grooming? _No_

How physically challenging? _No_

_____

Need to be reminded to bathe/groom? _No_

5-MINUTE MEMORY CHECK ___Car (1/3)_

DAILY SCHEDULE (What do you do in a typical day? (e.g., chores, shopping, laundry, yard work, repairs, hobbies, employment, school). List in time order.

Time	Activity
7:00	Get up, hygiene, bath, dressed, children off to school, spouse to work
8:00	Breakfast independently
9:00	Go for short walk
10:00	Look at newspaper, difficulties reading/concentrating
10:30	Crossword puzzle
11:00	Yard work (does not want to go shopping, sometimes will go with spouse)
12:00	Lunch
1:00	Nap (or speech and physical therapy 2x/week)
3:30	Children home from school, watch TV
5:00	Spouse home from work, cook dinner together usually
6:00	TV with family
8:00	Sit on porch
10:00	Watch news
11:00	Bed ½ hr to fall asleep wake up 2–3x/night

Notes ___Prefers to stay at home. Previously much more socially active._

_____

3.6

How do you financially care for basic needs? _Disability insurance and spouse's income._

Pick one or more activity regularly performed. Note concentration/persistence/pace. _____
Reading; must re-read each paragraph. Driving; gets lost easily. Chores; Often forgets tasks
half-way through. Double the time necessary. Computers (previous career); can no longer program.

Describe any incidents of withdrawal when symptoms increase. Note frequency/duration.

Increased social withdrawal as insight into memory/concentration increases.

How many household chores do you perform? (e.g., mow, rake, shovel, gardening, wash dishes, load dishwasher, laundry, mop, sweeping, make beds, clean bathrooms, vacuuming, painting, heavy lifting, etc.)
No physical restrictions, but as complexity increases, level of anxiety and confusion increases.

Do you
___Drive car   ___Run errands   ___Use public transportation
___Take taxicab   ___Go to post office   ___Go shopping
_X_ Walk places   _X_ Other _Will go in car with spouse_

Who pays the bills? _Spouse_   Who handles the finances? _Spouse_
Savings account _X_   Checking account _X_   Figure change _Not sure_

Involved in various activities? (e.g., movies, eat out, meetings, dancing, go for walks, biking, hunting, fishing, sports, draw, paint, take care of pets) _Fishing, short walks, puzzles_

Ability to concentrate on these? _Okay if familiar, poor if new or complex_
Write letters? _No_   How often? _____   Travel? _No_   How often? _____
Other activities (volunteering, religious meetings, AA, groups, etc.)   How often?
None

Ability to focus on these activities _____

3) Living situation
Describe living conditions (family, alone, crowded, functional, group home, etc.) _Describes family as_
supportive, but difficult for spouse due to increased responsibilities placed on her.

4) Ability to relate to others (e.g., aggressive, deferent, shy, defiant, avoidant, oppositional, normal)

Adults	_Avoids_	Authority figures	+
Teachers		Police	+
Peers	+	Family	+
Neighbors	+	Younger children	
Other			

Have best friend? _Yes, lifelong_   Group of friends? _Yes, but decreasing contact_
Activities with friend(s) _Currently some phone calls, fishing at times. Previously attended_
sports events.
How well did client relate (examiner, office personnel) during office visit? _Appeared somewhat_
anxious. Cooperative. Sat in far corner of waiting room.

5) Substance abuse (if applicable)

Detailed history and current information regarding substance abuse patterns.

Age of onset ___16___ Substances used historically _Beer, vodka_

History of usage _Teenager, occasional drinking from peer pressure. Increased usage in college,_
especially at exam time. During a few times of unemployment has noted periods of drunkenness
to escape the guilt feelings. A "slight buzz" has helped him feel more "sociable." Three months
after accident, increased use of alcohol. "I must drink if I go out in public." Drinks when his
family is not home. Usually able to hide his drinking. No desire to quit.

_____

_____

_____

_____

_____

Current substances used _____ _Vodka, beer_

Level of usage (how much) _____ _Up to 3 fifths/week + 12-pack of beer_

Frequency (how often) _____ _Daily_

Duration (length of episodes) _____ _2–3 hours_

Effects on functioning (impact on activities, interests, ability to relate, persistence/pace) _Notes effects_
in positive terms such as "less nervous"

_____

Reason(s) for usage ___ taste _X_ escape ___ self-medicate ___ addiction ___other _____

_X_Weekdays? What time(s) of day? _When family is not home_

___Weekends? What time(s) of day? _____

_X_Alone _X_Home ___With others ___Bars ___Other _____

How often do you drink to the point of intoxication (or get high) in a given week?
One time/week on Wednesdays when spouse works until 8:00 and children go to grandmother's.

How many binges in a given year? _0_

Frequency/duration of binges _____ _0_

Describe treatment history and medical/social consequences of the abuse (e.g., DWIs, DTs and tremors,
blackouts, job loss, divorce, etc.) _No negative consequences to date, but increasing_
desire/need to drink. Beginning to feel physical need for alcohol, especially on weekends or when
with family in social situations.

_____

_____

_____

_____

_____

MENTAL STATUS EXAM

1) CLINICAL OBSERVATIONS
APPEARANCE

Posture	OK
Clothing	Casual, clean
Grooming	OK
Hair	OK
Nails	Trimmed
Health	Appeared normal
Demeanor	OK
Other	

ACTIVITY LEVEL

Mannerisms	OK
Tics	No
Agitated	Slightly; appeared frustrated about being evaluated
Hyperactivity	No
Picking	No
Limp	No
Rigid	Somewhat
Gestures	OK
Combative	No
Gait	Normal
Other	

SPEECH

Slow	Somewhat
Rapid	No
Pressured	Somewhat
Hesitant	Somewhat
Monotonous	No
Slurred	At times
Stuttering	Slightly
Mumbled	No
Echolalia	No
Neologisms	No
Vocabulary	Slightly below average; some searching for words previously known
Repetition	No
Details	Few; brief sentences
Pitch	OK
Volume	OK
Reaction time	Slightly delayed; usually hesitated before answering
Other	

ATTITUDE TOWARD EXAMINER

Cooperative	*Increased with rapport*
Ingratiating	*No*
Attentive	*Lost track a few times*
Interested	*Yes*
Frank	*Yes*
Defensive	*No*
Hostile	*No*
Playful	*No*
Evasive	*Not purposely*
Other	

2) STREAM OF CONSCIOUSNESS THOUGHT PROCESSES

Number of ideas	*OK*
Flight of ideas	*No*
Hesitancy	*Some*
Spontaneity	*OK*

RE: QUESTIONS ANSWERED

Relevance	*OK*
Cause/effect	*OK*
Coherent	*OK*
Logical	*OK*
Rambling	*No*
Evasive	*No*
Language	*Concordant with current Tx*
Speech	*OK*
Neologisms	*No*
Associations	*OK*
Loose	*No*
Clanging	*No*

3) THOUGHT CONTENT
PREOCCUPATIONS

Obsessions	*No*
Compulsions	*No*
Phobias	*Increasing level of social anxiety*
Suicide	*Denies ideations or previous attempts*
Homicide	*No*
Antisocial	*No*
Other	

THOUGHT DISTURBANCES

DELUSIONS

Persecutory _____No_____

Somatic _____No_____

Grandeur _____No_____

IDEAS OF REFERENCE

Controlled by others _____No_____

Thought broadcasting _____No_____

Antisocial _____No_____

Validity _____OK_____

Content _____OK_____

Mood _____OK_____

Bizarre _____No_____

Other _____No_____

HALLUCINATIONS/ILLUSIONS

Example: Do you hear voices? Where? When do you recognize them? What do they say? Do you see things that other people do not see? Do you experience peculiar tastes or smells? Are they agreeable or disagreeable? Are there strange sensations or feelings, such as electricity going through the body or odd sexual sensations?

Voices _____No_____

Visions _____No_____

Content _____No_____

Setting _____No_____

Sensory system _____No_____

Other _____

DEPERSONALIZATION

Detachment _____No_____

OBSERVATIONS/EVIDENCE OF THOUGHT DISORDER
_____None_____

4) AFFECT/MOOD

A) Frequency/Intensity in daily life (Give specific examples of impairments/strengths, frequency, duration.)

Affection toward others _Shows normal affection toward family members._

_____

Anger: Anger management issues, property destruction, explosive behaviors, assaultive behaviors. How does the client act on anger? _____ _No anger management problems._

_____

Panic attacks: 4 or more, (abrupt development of: palpitations, sweating, trembling, shortness of breath, feeling of choking, chest pain, nausea, dizziness, light-headedness, derealization, fear of losing control, fear of dying, numbness, chills, or hot flashes) _Emerging symptoms of PA's. When in new situations feels short of breath,_ _sweaty, and palpitations. Onset, 3 months ago. Frequency, most of time when leaving house_ _or property or involved in new situations. Duration, 5–30 minutes._

Anxiety: Generalized Anxiety Disorder (GAD): 3 or more, most of time, past 6 months (restlessness, easily fatigued, concentration difficulty, irritability, muscle tension, sleep disturbance) _____
Not anxious in familiar environments. No Hx of anxiety disorder.

_____

Depression: Major Depressive Episode (MDE): 5 or more (usual depressed mood, anhedonia, weight +/– 5%/month with daily appetite +/–,.sleep +/–, psychomotor +/-, fatigue, worthlessness/guilt, concentration difficulty, death/suicidal ideation)
_____ _Denies Sx of clinical depression. Did not appear depressed._

_____

_____

Crying spells _____ _No_ _____

Suicidal _____ _No_ _____

_____

Withdrawal _____ _Increasing in past few months_ _____
Irritability _____ _Denies_ _____
Other _____

Mania: 3+ (Grandiosity, low sleep, talkativeness, flight of ideas, distractibility, goals/agitation, excessive pleasure)
_____ _No_ _____

Range of affect   ___Broad (normal)   _X_ Restricted (reduced)
    ___Blunted (severely reduced)   ___Flat (few/no signs)

Appropriateness of affect   _X_ Concordant   ___Discordant   with speech/ideas.
Predominant mood _____ _Somewhat anxious_ _____
Fluctuations _____ _No_ _____
Affective expression _____ _Moderate_ _____

5) SENSORIUM/COGNITION

A) Reality Contact (How in touch with reality is the client?)
_____*Yes*_____

Able to hold normal conversation? _X_ Yes ___ No

B) Orientation X3 _X_ Time _X_ Place _X_ Person Notes _____

C) Concentration

Attention to tasks/conversation; distractibility _*Asked to have a few questions repeated*_
Count to 40 by 3s, beginning at 1. (1, 4, 7, 10, 13, 16, 19, 22, 25, 28, 31, 34, 37, 40)
Number of errors __*6*__   Time between digit __*6–10 sec's.*__   Other _____
Notes ___*Below average*_____

Count backwards by 7s from 100. (100, 93, 86, 79, 72, 65, 58, 51, 44, 37, 30, 23, 16, 9, 2)
Number of errors __*Most*__   Time between digits __*15+*__   Other _____
Notes ___*Gave up after 5 incorrect answers*_____

$5 + 8 =$ _*13*_ $7 \times 4 =$ _*28*_ $12 \times 6 =$ _*72*_ $65 \div 5 =$ _*(15)*_   Timing ___*Slow*___

Digits forward and backward (Average adult: Fwd. = 5 – 7   Bwd. = 4 – 6)
Fwd. 42 _X_   368 _X_   6385 _X_   96725 _N_   864972 ___   5739481 ___   31749852 ___
Bwd. 91 _X_   582 _X_   9147 _No_   63892 ___   839427 ___   7392641 ___   49521863 ___
Fwd. = _5_   Bwd. = _3_   Evaluation: _X_ Below average   ___ Average   ___ Above average

D) Memory
Remote Memory
Childhood data: Schools attended _____*X*_____
                         Teachers' names/faces _*No names/some faces*_
                         Street grew up on _____*X*_____
                         Mother's maiden name _*X*_

Significant historical events (e.g., Kennedy's death, Challenger tragedy, Reagan shot) _*Recalls activities of day*_
___*when President Kennedy was shot.*_____

Recent Memory
Activities past few months ____*Vague—"trying to keep busy"*_____
Past few days ____*Vague—"Putzing around the house"*_____
Activities past weekend ____*Stayed home*_____
Yesterday (events, meals, etc.) _*Not sure*_____
Today (events, meals, etc.) ____*Cereal for breakfast*_____

30-MINUTE MEMORY CHECK _*Car (1/3)*_____

Comments re: Memory ___*Long-term intact; concerns with short-term and immediate*___
_____
_____

E) Information (knowledge of current events)

Does the client   _X_ read newspaper?   How often? _1x/week, ½ hour_

             _X_ TV/radio news?   How often? _Daily TV news_

Name current local/national news   _Vague—"Crime," "Weather," "Politics"_

President's name   _X_   3 Large cities   _X_

F) Judgment

"First one in theater to see smoke and fire"   _Get out, then yell "Fire"_

"Find stamped envelope in street"   _Mail it_

G) Abstractive Capacity

PROVERBS   INTERPRETATION GIVEN

"Rolling stone gathers no moss" _____

"Early bird catches the worm"   _First one up gets the best_

"Strike while the iron is hot" _____

Abstract vs. concrete interpretations   _Abstract_

H) Insight (awareness of issues; what level?)

__Complete denial   __Slight awareness   __Awareness, but blames others

_X_ Intellectual insight, but few changes likely   __Emotional insight, understanding, changes can occur

Comment on client's level of insight to problems: _____

_____

I) Intellectual level/Education/IQ estimate

Education level: Formal _16 years_   Informal _Coursework_

Intelligence _Above average (by history)_

General knowledge _Moderate_

Career background _Computer programmer_

6) PERSONALITY DISORDER (Fully describe any evidence of a personality disorder)

    _No_

_____

_____

_____

_____

_____

7) SOMATOFORM DISORDER (**4 pain Sx:** head, abdomen, back, joints, extremities, chest, rectum, menstruation, sexual intercourse, urination; **2 gastrointestinal Sx:** nausea, bloating, vomiting, diarrhea, food intolerance; **1 pseudoneurological Sx:** conversion Sx impaired coordination, aphonia, urinary retention, hallucinations, loss of touch or pain sensation, double vision, blindness, deafness, seizures, dissociative Sx, loss of consciousness)

History of problem   _Denies Sx_

_____

Primary/secondary gain_____

Family response _____

Selective nature of Sx _____

Observations (pain, fatigue, gait, dizziness) _____

Comments _____

3.14

8) ASSESSMENT

Summary and diagnostic findings (Tie together history and mental status findings and relate to diagnosis. Include onset of current Sx of the condition and how far back it goes. Include prognosis.)

Denies previous mental health issues. Increased anxiety and memory/concentration problems since auto accident 1 year ago, resulting in lost job and social anxiety. Emerging panic attacks. Few/no social interaction initiations. Difficulties coping with new situations/people. Problems with memory functioning since accident. Gets lost easily. Physical improvements noted. Hx of substance abuse in stressful times in his life. Current increase in alcohol consumption to escape current problems and to alleviate social anxiety. Excessive use of alcohol for past 6 months. Admits physical dependence. Timing of drinking controlled by family's schedule.
WAIS-R High average range. See protocol.
WMSR (Wechsler Memory Scale—Revised) Below average. See protocol.
Significant concerns in memory impairment, alcohol abuse; memory, panic symptoms increasing.
Prognosis: guarded

Axis I	*294.0 Amnesic disorder due to closed head injury (Provisional)*
	300.22 R/O Panic with agoraphobia
	303.90 Alcohol dependence, early onset, Hx of abuse
Axis II	*799.99 No Dx*
Axis III	*Defer to physician*
Axis IV	*Unemployment, changes in functioning at home*
Axis V	*Current GAF = 50; Past year 65*

9) ABILITY TO HANDLE FUNDS   (REQUIRED SSI STATEMENT)

Client's ability to handle funds is in his/her best interest. For Social Security purposes, incapacity means adult (18+) is dependent on others to provide protection of interests in daily needs (food, shelter, clothing).

+

10) MEDICAL SOURCES STATEMENT   (REQUIRED SSI STATEMENT)

Comment on, based on your findings, the client's ability to concentrate on and understand directions, carry out tasks with reasonable persistence and pace, respond appropriately to coworkers and supervisors, and tolerate the stresses in the workplace.

Concentration, moderate ability. Understands basic directions; poor understanding of complex directions. Difficulties responding to coworkers/supervisors due to increased social anxiety.
Not able to handle stress in work place at this time.

Adult Psychological Evaluation

Client's Name _____ Date _____

SSN _____ DOB _____

Allegations (Presenting problem) _____

Collateral information by _____ Relationship _____

Other Information _____

A. PHYSICAL DESCRIPTION

Identification given _____ Gender _____ Age _____

Race _____   Height _____   Weight _____   Eyes _____   Hair _____

Other descriptors of appearance _____

B. HISTORY

1) Signs and symptoms

Purpose of evaluation. Specific concerns and functional impairments (e.g., social, occupational, affective, cognitive, memory, physical, etc.).

_____

_____

_____

_____

_____

Impacts of impairments on functioning _____

_____

_____

As seen by professional _____

_____

2) History of present illness

Onset of impairment _____

Previous diagnoses (by whom?) _____

_____

Course of illness   __ Improving   __ Stable   __ Deteriorating

_____

_____

_____

_____

Events affecting frequency and duration _____
_____
_____

Precipitating factors (emotional, environmental, social) _____
_____
_____

Previous/current mental health treatment (and its effectiveness) _____
_____
_____

Current/previous medications _____
_____

Compliance? _____   Effectiveness _____

Hospitalizations/treatment _____
_____

Current special services (social, educational, legal) _____
_____
_____

NOTE AND RESOLVE ANY DISCREPANCIES BETWEEN INFORMATION GIVEN AND WHAT
RECORDS INDICATE. _____
_____
_____

BEGIN 5/30-MINUTE MEMORY CHECK_____

Activities of Daily Living
C. CURRENT LEVEL OF DAILY FUNCTIONING
1) Current hobbies, interests, and scope of interests

Hobby/interest	How persistently is it followed?	
	Frequency	Duration
_____	_____	_____
_____	_____	_____
_____	_____	_____
_____	_____	_____

Realistic, appropriate, compare to previous functioning _____
_____
_____

2) Activities

Do you live in a ___ house ___ apartment ___ townhouse ___ condo ___ mobile home

Who else lives there? (relationships, ages) _____

_____

What kinds of things do you usually eat for

Breakfast _____

Lunch _____

Dinner _____

Do you have physical problems in bathing/grooming? _____

How physically challenging? _____

_____

Need to be reminded to bathe/groom? _____

5-MINUTE MEMORY CHECK _____

DAILY SCHEDULE (What do you do in a typical day? (e.g., chores, shopping, laundry, yard work, repairs, hobbies, employment, school). List in time order.

Time	Activity
_____	_____
_____	_____
_____	_____
_____	_____
_____	_____
_____	_____
_____	_____
_____	_____
_____	_____
_____	_____
_____	_____
_____	_____
_____	_____
_____	_____
_____	_____
_____	_____
_____	_____
_____	_____

Notes _____

_____

3.18

How do you financially care for basic needs? _____
_____

Pick one or more activity regularly performed. Note concentration/persistence/pace. _____
_____
_____

Describe any incidents of withdrawal when symptoms increase. Note frequency/duration.
_____

How many household chores do you perform? (e.g., mow, rake, shovel, gardening, wash dishes, load dishwasher, laundry, mop, sweeping, make beds, clean bathrooms, vacuuming, painting, heavy lifting, etc.)
_____
_____

Do you
___Drive car   ___Run errands   ___Use public transportation
___Take taxicab   ___Go to post office   ___Go shopping
___Walk places   ___Other _____

Who pays the bills? _____   Who handles the finances? _____
Savings account _____   Checking account _____   Figure change _____

Involved in various activities? (e.g., movies, eat out, meetings, dancing, go for walks, biking, hunting, fishing, sports, draw, paint, take care of pets) _____
_____

Ability to concentrate on these? _____
Write letters? _____ How often? _____   Travel? _____   How often? _____
Other activities (volunteering, religious meetings, AA, groups, etc.)   How often?
_____   _____
_____   _____
_____   _____

Ability to focus on these activities _____
_____

3) Living situation
Describe living conditions (family, alone, crowded, functional, group home, etc.) _____
_____

4) Ability to relate to others (e.g., aggressive, deferent, shy, defiant, avoidant, oppositional, normal)
_____

Adults _____   Authority figures _____
Teachers _____   Police _____
Peers _____   Family _____
Neighbors _____   Younger children _____
Other _____
Have best friend? _____   Group of friends? _____
Activities with friend(s) _____

How well did client relate (examiner, office personnel) during office visit? _____
_____

5) Substance abuse (if applicable)

Detailed history and current information regarding substance abuse patterns.

Age of onset _____ Substances used historically _____

History of usage _____

_____

_____

_____

_____

_____

_____

_____

_____

_____

_____

Current substances used _____

Level of usage (how much) _____

Frequency (how often) _____

Duration (length of episodes) _____

Effects on functioning (impact on activities, interests, ability to relate, persistence/pace) _____

_____

_____

Reason(s) for usage ___ taste ___ escape ___ self-medicate ___ addiction ___ other _____

___Weekdays? What time(s) of day? _____

___Weekends? What time(s) of day? _____

___Alone ___Home ___With others ___Bars ___Other _____

How often do you drink to the point of intoxication (or get high) in a given week?

_____

How many binges in a given year? _____

Frequency/duration of binges _____

Describe treatment history and medical/social consequences of the abuse (e.g., DWIs, DTs and tremors, blackouts, job loss, divorce, etc.) _____

_____

_____

_____

_____

_____

_____

_____

_____

MENTAL STATUS EXAM

1) CLINICAL OBSERVATIONS

APPEARANCE

Posture _____

Clothing _____

Grooming _____

Hair _____

Nails _____

Health _____

Demeanor _____

Other _____

ACTIVITY LEVEL

Mannerisms _____

Tics _____

Agitated _____

Hyperactivity _____

Picking _____

Limp _____

Rigid _____

Gestures _____

Combative _____

Gait _____

Other _____

SPEECH

Slow _____

Rapid _____

Pressured _____

Hesitant _____

Monotonous _____

Slurred _____

Stuttering _____

Mumbled _____

Echolalia _____

Neologisms _____

Vocabulary _____

Repetition _____

Details _____

Pitch _____

Volume _____

Reaction time _____

Other _____

ATTITUDE TOWARD EXAMINER

Cooperative _____

Ingratiating _____

Attentive _____

Interested _____

Frank _____

Defensive _____

Hostile _____

Playful _____

Evasive _____

Other _____

2) STREAM OF CONSCIOUSNESS THOUGHT PROCESSES

Number of ideas _____

Flight of ideas _____

Hesitancy _____

Spontaneity _____

RE: QUESTIONS ANSWERED

Relevance _____

Cause/effect _____

Coherent _____

Logical _____

Rambling _____

Evasive _____

Language _____

Speech _____

Neologisms _____

Associations _____

    Loose _____

    Clanging _____

3) THOUGHT CONTENT
PREOCCUPATIONS

Obsessions _____

Compulsions _____

Phobias _____

Suicide _____

Homicide _____

Antisocial _____

Other _____

THOUGHT DISTURBANCES

DELUSIONS

Persecutory _____

Somatic _____

Grandeur _____

IDEAS OF REFERENCE

Controlled by others _____

Thought broadcasting _____

Antisocial _____

Validity _____

Content _____

Mood _____

Bizarre _____

Other _____

HALLUCINATIONS/ILLUSIONS

Example: Do you hear voices? Where? When do you recognize them? What do they say? Do you see things that other people do not see? Do you experience peculiar tastes or smells? Are they agreeable or disagreeable? Are there strange sensations or feelings, such as electricity going through the body or odd sexual sensations?

Voices _____

_____

Visions _____

_____

Content _____

Setting _____

Sensory system _____

Other _____

DEPERSONALIZATION

Detachment _____

_____

OBSERVATIONS/EVIDENCE OF THOUGHT DISORDER

_____

_____

_____

_____

_____

4) AFFECT/MOOD

A) Frequency/Intensity in daily life (Give specific examples of impairments/strengths, frequency, duration.)

Affection toward others _____

_____

Anger: Anger management issues, property destruction, explosive behaviors, assaultive behaviors. How does the client act on anger?_____

_____

Panic attacks: 4 or more (abrupt development of: palpitations, sweating, trembling, shortness of breath, feeling of choking, chest pain, nausea, dizziness, light-headedness, derealization, fear of losing control, fear of dying, numbness, chills, or hot flashes) _____

_____

_____

Anxiety: GAD: 3 or more, most of time, past 6 months (restlessness, easily fatigued, concentration difficulty, irritability, muscle tension, sleep disturbance) _____

_____

_____

Depression: MDE: 5 or more (usual depressed mood, anhedonia, weight +/– 5%/month with daily appetite +/–, sleep +/–, psychomotor +/–, fatigue, worthlessness/guilt, concentration difficulty, death/suicidal ideation)

_____

_____

_____

_____

Crying spells _____

Suicidal _____

_____

Withdrawal _____
Irritability _____
Other _____

Mania: 3+ (Grandiosity, low sleep, talkativeness, flight of ideas, distractibility, goals/agitation, excessive pleasure)

_____

Range of affect   ___Broad (normal)   ___Restricted (reduced)

                         ___Blunted (severely reduced)   ___Flat (few/no signs)

Appropriateness of affect   __Concordant   ___Discordant   with speech/ideas.

Predominant mood _____

Fluctuations _____

Affective expression _____

5) SENSORIUM/COGNITION

A) Reality Contact (How in touch with reality is the client?)

_____

Able to hold normal conversation?   __ Yes   __ No

B) Orientation X3   __ Time   __ Place   __ Person   Notes _____

C) Concentration

Attention to tasks/conversation; distractibility _____

Count to 40 by 3s, beginning at 1.   (1, 4, 7, 10, 13, 16, 19, 22, 25, 28, 31, 34, 37, 40)

Number of errors _____   Time between digit _____   Other _____

Notes _____

Count backwards by 7s from 100.   (100, 93, 86, 79, 72, 65, 58, 51, 44, 37, 30, 23, 16, 9, 2)

Number of errors _____   Time between digits _____   Other _____

Notes   _____

5 + 8 = _____   7 x 4 = _____   12 x 6 = _____   65 ÷ 5 = _____   Timing _____

Digits forward and backward (Average adult: Fwd. = 5 – 7   Bwd. = 4 – 6)

Fwd.	42__	368__	6385__	96725__	864972__	5739481__	31749852__
Bwd.	91__	582__	9147__	63892__	839427__	7392641__	49521863__

Fwd. = ____   Bwd. = ____   Evaluation: __Below average   __Average   __Above average

D) Memory
Remote Memory

Childhood data: Schools attended _____

Teachers' names/faces _____

Street grew up on _____

Mother's maiden name _____

Significant historical events (e.g., Kennedy's death, Challenger tragedy, Reagan shot)_____

_____

Recent Memory

Activities past few months _____

Past few days _____

Activities past weekend _____

Yesterday (events, meals, etc.) _____

Today (events, meals, etc.) _____

30-MINUTE MEMORY CHECK _____

Comments re: Memory _____

_____

_____

E) Information (knowledge of current events)

Does the client ___read newspaper?   How often?_____

              ___TV/radio news?   How often?_____

Name current local/national news _____

President's name _____ 3 Large cities _____

F) Judgment

"First one in theater to see smoke and fire" _____

"Find stamped envelope in street" _____

G) Abstractive Capacity

PROVERBS   INTERPRETATION GIVEN

"Rolling stone gathers no moss" _____

"Early bird catches the worm" _____

"Strike while the iron is hot" _____

Abstract vs. concrete interpretations _____

H) Insight (awareness of issues; what level?)

__Complete denial   __Slight awareness   __Awareness, but blames others

__Intellectual insight, but few changes likely   __Emotional insight, understanding, changes can occur

Comment on client's level of insight to problems: _____

_____

I) Intellectual level/Education/IQ estimate

Education level: Formal _____   Informal_____

Intelligence _____

General knowledge _____

Career background _____

6) PERSONALITY DISORDER (Fully describe any evidence of a personality disorder)

_____

_____

_____

_____

_____

_____

7) SOMATOFORM DISORDER (**4 pain Sx:** head, abdomen, back, joints, extremities, chest, rectum, menstruation, sexual intercourse, urination; **2 gastrointestinal Sx:** nausea, bloating, vomiting, diarrhea, food intolerance; **1 pseudoneurological Sx:** conversion Sx impaired coordination, aphonia, urinary retention, hallucinations, loss of touch or pain sensation, double vision, blindness, deafness, seizures, dissociative Sx, loss of consciousness)

History of problem _____

_____

Primary/secondary gain_____

Family response _____

Selective nature of Sx _____

Observations (pain, fatigue, gait, dizziness) _____

Comments _____

8) ASSESSMENT

Summary and diagnostic findings (Tie together history and mental status findings and relate to diagnosis. Include onset of current Sx of the condition and how far back it goes. Include prognosis.)

_____
_____
_____
_____
_____
_____
_____
_____
_____
_____
_____
_____
_____

Axis I   _____
                  _____

Axis II   _____
                  _____

Axis III   _____
Axis IV   _____
Axis V   _____

9) ABILITY TO HANDLE FUNDS   (REQUIRED SSI STATEMENT)

Client's ability to handle funds is in his/her best interest. For Social Security purposes, incapacity means adult (18+) is dependent on others to provide protection of interests in daily needs (food, shelter, clothing).

_____
_____

10) MEDICAL SOURCES STATEMENT   (REQUIRED SSI STATEMENT)

Comment on, based on your findings, the client's ability to concentrate on and understand directions, carry out tasks with reasonable persistence and pace, respond appropriately to coworkers and supervisors, and tolerate the stresses in the workplace.

_____
_____
_____
_____
_____

Child Psychological Evaluation

Client's Name ___Christine Watters___ Date ___4-6-97___
SSN ___999-98-9999___ DOB ___3-6-91___ Age ___6-1___ Gender ___F___
Allegations (Presenting problem) ___Conduct problems at home and school___
Collateral information by ___Lisa Watters___ Relationship ___Mother___

(PARENT OR CAREGIVER USUALLY REMAINS IN INTERVIEW UNTIL MSE)

A. PHYSICAL DESCRIPTION
Identification given ___None___
Race _Afr-Am_ Height _4-4_ Weight _64_ Eyes _Br_ Hair _Bl_
Other descriptors of appearance _____

B. HISTORY
1) Signs and symptoms
Purpose of evaluation. Specific concerns and functional impairments (e.g., social, academic, affective, cognitive, memory, physical, etc.).
ADHD evaluation. Several reports from school indicating not finishing 50% of school tasks, not sitting still in school, disruptive, and not paying attention. Must be reminded several times to do any tasks at home. Falling behind in school. School is considering Emotional/Behavior Disorder (EBD) classes, if no improvements.

Impacts of impairments on functioning _Problems socially, and behaviorally in school with peers, sometimes teased by children of same age for immature behaviors. Falling increasingly behind in academics._

As seen by professional _Appeared fidgety and hyperactive. Moderate attention span. Got out of chair several times. Not initially interested in being interviewed, but became more compliant._

2) History of present illness
Onset of impairment _Parents noticed hyperactive behaviors since about age 3. Several comments from preschool teachers re: not focusing and always on the go. Parents thought she would "grow out of it."_
Previous diagnoses (by whom?) _____
None

Course of illness __ Improving __Stable _X_ Deteriorating
Since beginning of school year continued hyperactivity, but increasing defiance and problems appropriately socializing with classmates.

Events affecting frequency and duration *Situations in which she does not receive 1–1 attention.*

Precipitating factors (e.g., emotional, environmental, social) *When not center of atteniton may have temper tantrums.*

Previous/current mental health treatment (and its effectiveness) *No Hx of MH Tx.*

Current/previous medications *None*

Compliance? _____ Effectiveness _____

Hospitalizations/treatment *No Hx*

Current special services (e.g., social, educational, legal) *Previous Head Start. School considering special education for EBD.*

NOTE AND RESOLVE ANY DISCREPANCIES BETWEEN INFORMATION GIVEN AND WHAT RECORDS INDICATE. *Mother's descriptions seem concordant with observations.*

BEGIN 5/30-MINUTE MEMORY CHECK *Memorize cat/dog/rabbit*

ACTIVITIES OF DAILY LIVING

C. CURRENT LEVEL OF DAILY FUNCTIONING
1) Current hobbies, interests, and scope of interests

Hobby/interest	How persistently is it followed?	
	Frequency	Duration
Coloring	*Daily*	*5–10-min. intervals.*
TV/video games	*Daily*	*3–4 hours*
Play outdoors	*Daily/weekends*	*varies*

Realistic, appropriate, compare to previous functioning *Normal range of behaviors*

2) Activities

Do you live in a $\underline{X}$ house __ apartment __ townhouse __ condo __ mobile home

Who else lives there? (relationships, ages) _Both parents; 1 sister, 10; 1 brother, 4_

3) Living situation

Describe living conditions (family, alone, crowded, functional, group home, etc.) _Functional family._
Shares room with sister, age 10.

4) Ability to relate to others (e.g., aggressive, deferent, shy, defiant, avoidant, oppositional, normal)

Adults	_Ignores_	Authority figures	_OK_
Teachers	_Tries to cooperate_	Police	
Peers	_Teased by them_	Family	_Normal range of rivalry_
Neighbors	_OK_	Younger children	_+_

Other _____

Have best friend? _Yes_ Group of friends? _No_

Activities with friend(s) _Plays in park. Friend is one year younger._

How well did client relate (examiner, office personnel) **during office visit?** _Cooperated, but hyperactive_
and moderate attention span during interview, average attention span when high interest in the tasks.

5-MINUTE MEMORY CHECK _Cat, dog (2/3)_

DAILY SCHEDULE (What child does in a typical day: chores, TV, play, yard work, hobbies, employment, school). List in time order.

Time	Activity
	Typical School Day
_6:30_	_Get up. Dress independently (with several reminders—prefers to play)_
	Mother prompts her to get ready for school. Hygiene independently
_7:45_	_Catch school bus._
_8:30_	_School, 1st grade. Mainstream classes. Breakfast & lunch at school._
_3:30_	_Home, change clothes independently. Usually no homework. If good weather will_
	play outside until dinner; otherwise will play video games or watch TV.
_5:30_	_Dinner with family. Eats very quickly. Won't sit still at dinner table._
_6:00_	_Play outside. Enjoys going to park across street with friend._
_7:30_	_Home, TV. Rarely completes chores assigned, or does "poor job."_
	Mother states she is "always on the go" and "climbing the walls."
_9:00_	_Ready for bed, but may not fall asleep for 1–2 hours due to "playfulness."_
	Wakes up 1–2x/night. Toilet trained.

Notes _____

5) Substance abuse (if applicable)

Detailed history and current information regarding substance abuse patterns.

Age of onset _____ Substances used historically _____

History of usage _____ NA _____

_____
_____
_____
_____
_____
_____

6) Self-help skills (Describe child's ability and assistance needed)

Dressing _____ OK _____

Grooming _____ OK _____

Feeding self _____ OK _____

Avoiding dangers _ *Often runs into the street w/o looking. Often gets hurt "playing too hard."* _

Independent activities outside the home _ *Plays in park only.* _____

Making change ($) _____ NA _____

Taking the bus _____ NA _____

7) Concentration, persistence, and pace (ages 3–18)

(Describe ability to concentrate, attend, persist, and complete tasks in a timely manner.) _ *Home: Mother* _
describes problems at home staying on task due to hyperactivity. Seems to pay attention, but
has difficulties sitting still. Interview: Maintained conversation but hurried through most
tasks impulsively.

D) DEVELOPMENTAL MILESTONES

Pregnancy and delivery _X_ Normal ____ Problems (describe)_____
_____

Behavior	Age	Comments
Walking	13 m	All in normal range
Talking	20 m	
Toilet trained	4 y	

AGE GROUP OF CHILD __A (0–3) __B (3–6) _X_C (6–16) __D (16–18) Fill in for appropriate age group. (Provide specific information on how the child's symptoms impact performance of age-appropriate developmental tasks and functional capacity.)

A) Birth to 3 years

Locomotion (e.g., crawling, walking, sitting up, pulling oneself into an upright position, etc.)
_____
_____

Language (e.g., vocalization, imitative sounds, talking, receptive skills, ability to follow commands, etc.)
_____
_____

Gross motor competence (e.g., reaching, throwing, jumping, grasping, pedaling a tricycle, etc.)

_____

_____

Fine motor competence (pincer grip, grasp, colors, uses pencils, reaches for objects, etc.)

_____

_____

Behavioral-social (e.g., excessive crying, hyperactivity, fear response to separation, aggressiveness, temper outbursts, lethargy, inability to bond, autistic features, efforts at toilet training, ability to relate to peers, siblings, parents, etc.)

_____

_____

_____

B) 3 to 6 years

Locomotion (describe any abnormalities as listed above, describe development of competency)

_____

_____

Communication (speech development, ability to form sentences, clarity of speech, expressive skills, receptive skills, ability to communicate needs, ability to respond to commands, ability to follow simple directions)

_____

_____

_____

Motor (Describe any abnormalities in fine or gross motor activity, child's ability to use scissors, color within lines, copy simple designs such as circle, square. Include observations of any impairments in coordination and/or balance.)

_____

_____

Social/emotional (toilet training, aggressiveness, hyperactivity, ability to play with others, to share with others, to separate from caregivers, competency in feeding, dressing, and grooming skills, temper outbursts, night terrors, manifestations of anxiety, phobias, fear response to separation, observations of bizarre or aberrant behavior)

_____

_____

_____

Ability to concentrate, attend, persist, and complete tasks in a timely manner

_____

_____

_____

_____

C) 6 to 16 years

Locomotion (describe any abnormalities in walking, running, mobility)
Normal range

Communication (reading, writing, receptive and expressive language skills, speech)
Normal range

Motor skills (coordination, balance, perceptual motor skills, complex-integrated motor responses)
Normal range

Ability to concentrate, attend, persist, and complete tasks in a timely manner.
OK when interested or with 1–1 adult interaction. Concentration seems within normal limits.
Completes tasks impulsively. Any concentration issues seem secondary to hyperactivity.

D) 16 to 18 years

Locomotion (Describe any abnormalities in mobility.)

Communications (any abnormalities noted)

Social/emotional (relationships to peer group and to school authority figures). Any evidence of oppositional, rebellious, antisocial, aggressive behavior, withdrawal. Assess stress tolerance, potential employment, potential for substance abuse, impairment in reality testing. Comment on identity issues and development of body awareness.

Ability to concentrate, attend, persist, and complete tasks in a timely manner.

Other (Comment on any volunteer or after-school work, vocational training, jobs associated with the school program in terms of work, and ability to persist, complete tasks, and respond appropriately to supervision.)

PARENTS OR CAREGIVERS LEAVE INTERVIEW ROOM AT THIS TIME

MENTAL STATUS EXAM

1) CLINICAL OBSERVATIONS

APPEARANCE

Posture	OK
Clothing	Casual, clean, appropriate
Grooming	OK
Hair	Combed
Nails	Bitten
Health	Normal
Demeanor	Impulsive, active
Other	

ACTIVITY LEVEL

Mannerisms	OK
Tics	No
Agitated	When does not get own way
Hyperactivity	+++
Picking	No
Limp	No
Rigid	No
Gestures	None unusual
Combative	No
Gait	OK
Other	

SPEECH

Slow	No
Rapid	+
Pressured	No
Hesitant	No
Monotonous	No
Slurred	No
Stuttering	No
Mumbled	No
Echolalia	No
Neologisms	No
Vocabulary	Normal
Repetition	Often repeated to interviewer questions asked
Details	Normal
Pitch	OK
Volume	OK
Reaction time	Quick
Other	

ATTITUDE TOWARD EXAMINER

Cooperative	+
Ingratiating	No
Attentive	When interested in a task
Interested	At times
Frank	OK
Defensive	No
Hostile	No
Playful	Often
Evasive	No
Other	

2) STREAM OF CONSCIOUSNESS THOUGHT PROCESSES

Number of ideas	OK
Flight of ideas	No
Hesitancy	No
Spontaneity	OK

RE: QUESTIONS ANSWERED

Relevance	OK
Cause/effect	OK
Coherent	OK
Logical	OK
Rambling	No
Evasive	No
Language	OK
Speech	OK
Neologisms	No
Associations	OK
Loose	No
Clanging	No

3) THOUGHT CONTENT

Obsessions	No
Compulsions	No
Phobias	No
Suicide	No
Homicide	No
Antisocial	No
Other	

THOUGHT DISTURBANCES

DELUSIONS

Persecutory	*No*
Somatic	*No*
Grandeur	*No*

IDEAS OF REFERENCE

Controlled by others	*No*
Thought broadcasting	*No*
Antisocial	*No*
Validity	*OK*
Content	*OK*
Mood	*OK*
Bizarre	*No*
Other	

HALLUCINATIONS/ILLUSIONS

Example: Do you hear voices? Where? When do you recognize them? What do they say? Do you see things that other people do not see? Do you experience peculiar tastes or smells? Are they agreeable or disagreeable? Are there strange sensations or feelings, such as electricity going through the body or odd sexual sensations?

Voices	*No*
Visions	*No*
Content	*No*
Setting	*No*
Sensory system	*No*
Other	

DEPERSONALIZATION

Detachment	*No*

OBSERVATIONS/EVIDENCE OF THOUGHT DISORDER

No

4) AFFECT/MOOD

A) Frequency/Intensity in Daily Life (Give specific examples of impairments/strengths, frequency, duration.)

Affection _____
_____ OK _____

Anger: Anger management issues, property destruction, explosive behaviors, assaultive behaviors. How does the client act on anger? ___ *Growing concerns with temper tantrums* _____
 since beginning of 1st grade. No intentional property damage. _____

Panic Attacks: 4 or more (abrupt development of: palpitations, sweating, trembling, shortness of breath, feeling of choking, chest pain, nausea, dizziness, light-headedness, derealization, fear of losing control, fear of dying, numbness, chills, or hot flashes) ___ *None* _____
_____

Anxiety: GAD: 3 or more, most of time, past 6 months (restlessness, easily fatigued, concentration difficulty, irritability, muscle tension, sleep disturbance) ___ *No Sx of clinical anxiety* _____
_____

Depression: MDE: 5 or more (usual depressed mood, anhedonia, weight +/– 5%/month with daily appetite +/–, sleep +/–, psychomotor +/–, fatigue, worthlessness/guilt, concentration, death/suicidal ideation.
_____ *Denies* _____
_____
_____

Crying spells _____ *Age-appropriate number, usually when tantrumming* _____

Suicidal _____ *No* _____
_____

Withdrawal _____ *No* _____
Irritability _____ *Normal range* _____
Other _____

Mania: 3+ (Grandiosity, low sleep, talkativeness, flight of ideas, distractibility, goals/agitation, excessive pleasure)
_____ *No* _____

Range of affect   X Broad (normal)   ___Restricted (reduced)
                        ___Blunted (severely reduced)   ___Flat (few/no signs)

Appropriateness of affect   X Concordant   ___Discordant   __with speech/ideas.

Predominant mood _____
Fluctuations _____
Affective expression _____

B) Attention Span during Interview

Fidgety	_Usually_
Remains seated	_Difficult; out of seat several times_
Distracted	_When not interested in a task_
Blurts answers	_Usually_
Follows directions	_OK, but loses interest easily_
Shifts focus	_At times_
Talks excessively	_++_
Interrupts	_++_
Listens	_OK_
Impulsivity	_++_
Other	

C) Rule Out Clinical Syndromes

Anxiety disorders, depression, autism, pervasive developmental disorders, ADHD, autistic disorders, conduct/behavioral disorders, specific developmental disabilities, learning disorders, incipient psychotic process, and substance abuse.

Meets criteria for 314.01 ADHD, primarily hyperactive type. Sx include impulsivity, often interrupts, talks excessively, restlessness, difficulties remaining seated, constant need for 1–1 attention. Hyperactive behaviors interfering with academic functioning.

5) SENSORIUM/COGNITION   _Next Page_

YOUNGER CHILDREN: Provide a basic assessment of the following:

Consciousness (ability to concentrate, confusion, attending) _____

Orientation __Time __Place __Person Notes _____

Memory (recent, long-term, simple facts) _____

Estimated Intellectual Functioning _____

3.38

OLDER CHILDREN:

A) Reality Contact (How in touch with reality is the client?) _Age-appropriate_

_____

Able to hold normal conversation? _X_ Yes __No

B) Orientation X3 __Time __Place __Person Notes _Age-appropriate_

C) Concentration

Count to 40 by 3s, beginning at 1. (1, 4, 7, 10, 13, 16, 19, 22, 25, 28, 31, 34, 37, 40)
Number of errors _____ Time between digits _____ Other _____
Notes _____ NA _____

Count backwards by 7s from 100. (100, 93, 86, 79, 72, 65, 58, 51, 44, 37, 30, 23, 16, 9, 2)
Number of errors _____ Time between digits _____ Other _____
Notes _____ NA _____

$2 + 3 =$ _____ $3 - 2 =$ _____ $4 + 8 =$ _____ $9 + 12 =$ _____
$4 \times 3 =$ _____ $7 \times 4 =$ _____ $12 \times 6 =$ _____ $65 \div 5 =$ _____
  Not yet taught math. Able to count to 20 with no errors.

Digits forward and backward:
Fwd.   42 _X_   368 _X_   6385__   96725__   864972__   5739481__   31749852__
Bwd.   91 _No_   582__   9147__   63892__   839427__   7392641__   49521863__
Fwd. = _3_   Bwd. = _0_   Evaluation: _X_ Below average   __ Average   __Above average

D) Memory
Remote Memory
Childhood data: Schools attended _____ _Name of current school_ _____
                       Teachers' names/faces ____ _Current_ ____
                       Street grew up on _____ _(Knows current address/phone number)_ ____
                       Mother's maiden name ____ _Doesn't know_ ____

Significant historical events (e.g., Kennedy's death, Challenger tragedy, Reagan shot) _____
_____ _No_ _____

Recent Memory
Activities past few months _____
Past few days _____ _In school_ _____
Yesterday (events, meals, etc.) ___ _Some details of dinner_ _____
Today (events, meals, etc.) _____ _Breakfast_ _____

30-MINUTE MEMORY CHECK _Cat, dog (5 min = 2/3; 30 min = 2/3—Average)_

E) Information (knowledge of current events)

Does the client   ___read newspaper?   How often? _____ *NA*

                    ___TV/radio news?   How often? _____

Name current local/national news _____

President's name _____   Three large cities_____

F) Judgment

"First one in theater to see smoke and fire" _____

"Find stamped envelope in street" _____

G) Abstractive Capacity

PROVERBS   INTERPRETATION GIVEN

"Rolling stone gathers no moss" _____

"Early bird catches the worm" _____

"Strike while the iron is hot" _____

Abstract vs. concrete interpretations _____

H) Insight (awareness of issues; what level?)

__Complete denial   __Slight awareness   __Awareness, but blames others

__Intellectual insight, but few changes likely   __Emotional insight, understanding, changes can occur

Comment on client's level of insight to problems: _____

_____

I) Intellectual level/Education/IQ estimate

Grade in school __*1*__   Ever repeat a grade? *No*   Grades/Progress __*S's and I's*_____

Special education classes _____*No*_____

Intelligence _____*Avg*_____

General knowledge _____*Avg*_____

Selective nature of Sx _____*NA*_____

Observations (pain, fatigue, gait, dizziness) ____*Hyperactive*_____

Comments _____

J) Adverse Factors Affecting the Child's Ability to Function

(e.g., pain, side effects of meds, dysfunctional family, abuse, physical impairments, etc.)

No known adverse environmental factors or physical impairments.

_____

_____

_____

_____

_____

6) TESTING RESULTS

Wechsler Intelligence Scale for Children—3rd edition (WISC—3). Low normal range. See protocol.

7) ASSESSMENT

Summary and diagnostic findings   (Tie together history and mental status findings and relate to diagnosis. Include onset of current Sx of the condition and how far back it goes. Include prognosis.)

Problems in school and home with hyperactive behaviors. Increasing disruptive behaviors when not center of attention. Mother reports complaints from school due to interrupting, not staying seated, hyperactivity, talking excessively, impulsivity, and fidgetiness. Possible EBD referral for upcoming school year. Similar behaviors noted at home. Other children in school teasing her for below age level behaviors such as often getting out of seat in class. Only friend is one year younger. No mental health treatment or med history. No previous evaluation for ADHD. Appears to have average intellectual ability.

Axis I	*314.01 ADHD, primarily hyperactivity type*
Axis II	*Deferred*
Axis III	*Defer to physician*
Axis IV	*Few friends*
Axis V	*GAF = 75*

NOTE: FOR SOCIAL SECURITY DO NOT MAKE A STATEMENT AS TO WHETHER
THE CHILD IS DISABLED

Child Psychological Evaluation

Client's Name _____ Date _____

SSN _____ DOB _____ Age _____ Gender _____

Allegations (Presenting problem) _____

Collateral information by _____ Relationship _____

(PARENT OR CAREGIVER USUALLY REMAINS IN INTERVIEW UNTIL MSE)

A. PHYSICAL DESCRIPTION

Identification given _____

Race _____ Height _____ Weight _____ Eyes _____ Hair _____

Other descriptors of appearance _____

B. HISTORY

1) Signs and symptoms

Purpose of evaluation. Specific concerns and functional impairments (e.g., social, academic, affective, cognitive, memory, physical, etc.).

_____
_____
_____
_____

Impacts of impairments on functioning _____
_____
_____

As seen by professional _____
_____
_____

2) History of present illness

Onset of impairment _____
_____

Previous diagnoses (by whom?) _____
_____

Course of illness ___ Improving ___Stable ___Deteriorating
_____
_____
_____

Events affecting frequency and duration _____

_____

_____

Precipitating factors (e.g., emotional, environmental, social) _____

_____

_____

Previous/current mental health treatment (and its effectiveness) _____

_____

_____

_____

Current/previous medications _____

_____

Compliance? _____ Effectiveness _____

Hospitalizations/treatment _____

_____

Current special services (e.g., social, educational, legal)_____

_____

_____

NOTE AND RESOLVE ANY DISCREPANCIES BETWEEN INFORMATION GIVEN AND WHAT
RECORDS INDICATE. _____

_____

_____

BEGIN 5/30-MINUTE MEMORY CHECK _____

ACTIVITIES OF DAILY LIVING

C. CURRENT LEVEL OF DAILY FUNCTIONING
1) Current hobbies, interests, and scope of interests

Hobby/interest	How persistently is it followed?	
	Frequency	Duration
_____	_____	_____
_____	_____	_____
_____	_____	_____
_____	_____	_____

Realistic, appropriate, compare to previous functioning _____

_____

_____

3.43

2) Activities

Do you live in a __ house __ apartment __ townhouse __ condo __ mobile home

Who else lives there? (relationships, ages) _____

_____

3) Living situation

Describe living conditions (family, alone, crowded, functional, group home, etc.) _____

_____

_____

4) Ability to relate to others (e.g., aggressive, deferent, shy, defiant, avoidant, oppositional, normal)

_____

Adults _____ Authority figures _____

Teachers _____ Police _____

Peers _____ Family _____

Neighbors _____ Younger children _____

Other _____

Have best friend? _____ Group of friends? _____

Activities with friend(s) _____

_____

How well did client relate (examiner, office personnel) **during office visit?** _____

_____

5-MINUTE MEMORY CHECK _____

DAILY SCHEDULE (What child does in a typical day: chores, TV, play, yard work, hobbies, employment, school). List in time order.

Time	Activity
_____	_____
_____	_____
_____	_____
_____	_____
_____	_____
_____	_____
_____	_____
_____	_____
_____	_____
_____	_____
_____	_____
_____	_____
_____	_____
_____	_____
_____	_____
_____	_____

Notes _____

_____

5) Substance abuse (if applicable)

Detailed history and current information regarding substance abuse patterns.

Age of onset _____   Substances used historically _____

History of usage _____

_____

_____

_____

_____

_____

_____

_____

6) Self-help skills (Describe child's ability and assistance needed)

Dressing _____

Grooming _____

Feeding self _____

Avoiding dangers_____

Independent activities outside the home _____

Making change ($) _____

Taking the bus _____

7) Concentration, persistence, and pace (ages 3–18)

(Describe ability to concentrate, attend, persist, and complete tasks in a timely manner.) _____

_____

_____

_____

D) DEVELOPMENTAL MILESTONES

Pregnancy and delivery ____ Normal ____ Problems (describe)_____

_____

Behavior	Age	Comments
Walking	_____	_____
Talking	_____	_____
Toilet trained	_____	_____

AGE GROUP OF CHILD   __A (0–3) __B (3–6) __C (6–16) __D (16–18)   Fill in for appropriate age group. (Provide specific information on how the child's symptoms impact performance of age-appropriate developmental tasks and functional capacity.)

A) Birth to 3 years

Locomotion (e.g., crawling, walking, sitting up, pulling oneself into an upright position, etc.)

_____

_____

Language (e.g., vocalization, imitative sounds, talking, receptive skills, ability to follow commands, etc.)

_____

_____

Gross motor competence (e.g., reaching, throwing, jumping, grasping, pedaling a tricycle, etc.)

_____

_____

Fine motor competence (pincer grip, grasp, colors, uses pencils, reaches for objects, etc.)

_____

_____

Behavioral-social (e.g., excessive crying, hyperactivity, fear response to separation, aggressiveness, temper outbursts, lethargy, inability to bond, autistic features, efforts at toilet training, ability to relate to peers, siblings, parents, etc.)

_____

_____

_____

B) 3 to 6 years

Locomotion (describe any abnormalities as listed above, describe development of competency)

_____

_____

Communication (speech development, ability to form sentences, clarity of speech, expressive skills, receptive skills, ability to communicate needs, ability to respond to commands, ability to follow simple directions)

_____

_____

_____

Motor (Describe any abnormalities in fine or gross motor activity, child's ability to use scissors, color within lines, copy simple designs such as circle, square. Include observations of any impairments in coordination and/or balance.)

_____

_____

Social/emotional (toilet training, aggressiveness, hyperactivity, ability to play with others, to share with others, to separate from caregivers, competency in feeding, dressing, and grooming skills, temper outbursts, night terrors, manifestations of anxiety, phobias, fear response to separation, observations of bizarre or aberrant behavior)

_____

_____

_____

Ability to concentrate, attend, persist, and complete tasks in a timely manner

_____

_____

_____

_____

C) 6 to 16 years

Locomotion (describe any abnormalities in walking, running, mobility)

_____

_____

Communication (reading, writing, receptive and expressive language skills, speech)

_____

_____

Motor skills (coordination, balance, perceptual motor skills, complex-integrated motor responses)

_____

_____

Ability to concentrate, attend, persist, and complete tasks in a timely manner.

_____

_____

D) 16 to 18 years

Locomotion (Describe any abnormalities in mobility.)

_____

_____

Communications (any abnormalities noted)

_____

_____

Social/emotional (relationships to peer group and to school authority figures). Any evidence of oppositional, rebellious, antisocial, aggressive behavior, withdrawal. Assess stress tolerance, potential employment, potential for substance abuse, impairment in reality testing. Comment on identity issues and development of body awareness.

_____

_____

_____

Ability to concentrate, attend, persist, and complete tasks in a timely manner.

_____

_____

_____

Other (Comment on any volunteer or after-school work, vocational training, jobs associated with the school program in terms of work, and ability to persist, complete tasks, and respond appropriately to supervision.)

_____

_____

_____

_____

PARENTS OR CAREGIVERS LEAVE INTERVIEW ROOM AT THIS TIME

MENTAL STATUS EXAM

1) CLINICAL OBSERVATIONS

APPEARANCE

Posture   _____

Clothing   _____

Grooming _____

Hair   _____

Nails   _____

Health   _____

Demeanor _____

Other   _____

ACTIVITY LEVEL

Mannerisms _____

Tics   _____

Agitated   _____

Hyperactivity _____

Picking   _____

Limp   _____

Rigid   _____

Gestures   _____

Combative _____

Gait   _____

Other   _____

SPEECH

Slow   _____

Rapid   _____

Pressured _____

Hesitant   _____

Monotonous _____

Slurred   _____

Stuttering   _____

Mumbled   _____

Echolalia   _____

Neologisms _____

Vocabulary _____

Repetition _____

Details   _____

Pitch   _____

Volume   _____

Reaction time _____

Other   _____

ATTITUDE TOWARD EXAMINER

Cooperative _____

Ingratiating _____

Attentive _____

Interested _____

Frank _____

Defensive _____

Hostile _____

Playful _____

Evasive _____

Other _____

2) STREAM OF CONSCIOUSNESS THOUGHT PROCESSES

Number of ideas _____

Flight of ideas _____

Hesitancy _____

Spontaneity _____

RE: QUESTIONS ANSWERED

Relevance _____

Cause/effect _____

Coherent _____

Logical _____

Rambling _____

Evasive _____

Language _____

Speech _____

Neologisms _____

Associations _____

    Loose _____

    Clanging _____

3) THOUGHT CONTENT

Obsessions _____

Compulsions _____

Phobias _____

Suicide _____

Homicide _____

Antisocial _____

Other _____

THOUGHT DISTURBANCES

DELUSIONS

Persecutory   _____

Somatic   _____

Grandeur   _____

IDEAS OF REFERENCE

Controlled by others   _____

Thought broadcasting   _____

Antisocial   _____

Validity   _____

Content   _____

Mood   _____

Bizarre   _____

Other   _____

HALLUCINATIONS/ILLUSIONS

Example: Do you hear voices? Where? When do you recognize them? What do they say? Do you see things that other people do not see? Do you experience peculiar tastes or smells? Are they agreeable or disagreeable? Are there strange sensations or feelings, such as electricity going through the body or odd sexual sensations?

Voices   _____
               _____

Visions   _____
               _____

Content   _____

Setting   _____

Sensory system _____

Other   _____

DEPERSONALIZATION

Detachment   _____
               _____

OBSERVATIONS/EVIDENCE OF THOUGHT DISORDER

_____
_____
_____
_____
_____

4) AFFECT/MOOD

A) Frequency/Intensity in Daily Life (Give specific examples of impairments/strengths, frequency, duration.)

Affection _____

_____

Anger: Anger management issues, property destruction, explosive behaviors, assaultive behaviors. How does the client act on anger? _____

_____

Panic Attacks: 4 or more (abrupt development of: palpitations, sweating, trembling, shortness of breath, feeling of choking, chest pain, nausea, dizziness, light-headedness, derealization, fear of losing control, fear of dying, numbness, chills, or hot flashes)_____

_____

_____

Anxiety: GAD: 3 or more, most of time, past 6 months (restlessness, easily fatigued, concentration difficulty, irritability, muscle tension, sleep disturbance) _____

_____

_____

Depression: MDE: 5 or more (usual depressed mood, anhedonia, weight +/– 5%/month with daily appetite +/–, sleep +/–, psychomotor +/–, fatigue, worthlessness/guilt, concentration, death/suicidal ideation.

_____

_____

_____

_____

Crying spells _____

Suicidal _____

_____

Withdrawal _____

Irritability _____

Other _____

Mania: 3+ (Grandiosity, low sleep, talkativeness, flight of ideas, distractibility, goals/agitation, excessive pleasure)

_____

Range of affect   ___Broad (normal)   ___Restricted (reduced)
                         ___Blunted (severely reduced)   ___Flat (few/no signs)

Appropriateness of affect   __Concordant   ___Discordant   __with speech/ideas.

Predominant mood _____

Fluctuations _____

Affective expression _____

B) Attention Span during Interview

Fidgety _____

Remains seated _____

Distracted _____

Blurts answers _____

Follows directions _____

Shifts focus _____

Talks excessively _____

Interrupts _____

Listens _____

Impulsivity _____

Other _____

_____

C) Rule Out Clinical Syndromes

Anxiety disorders, depression, autism, pervasive developmental disorders, ADHD, autistic disorders, conduct/behavioral disorders, specific developmental disabilities, learning disorders, incipient psychotic process, and substance abuse.

_____

_____

_____

_____

_____

_____

_____

_____

_____

_____

5) SENSORIUM/COGNITION

YOUNGER CHILDREN: Provide a basic assessment of the following:

Consciousness (ability to concentrate, confusion, attending) _____

_____

_____

Orientation __Time __Place __Person Notes _____

Memory (recent, long-term, simple facts) _____

_____

Estimated Intellectual Functioning _____

_____

OLDER CHILDREN:

A) Reality Contact (How in touch with reality is the client?) _____

_____

Able to hold normal conversation?   __Yes   __No

B) Orientation X3   __Time   __Place   __Person   Notes_____

C) Concentration

Count to 40 by 3s, beginning at 1. (1, 4, 7, 10, 13, 16, 19, 22, 25, 28, 31, 34, 37, 40)
Number of errors _____   Time between digits _____   Other _____
Notes _____

Count backwards by 7s from 100. (100, 93, 86, 79, 72, 65, 58, 51, 44, 37, 30, 23, 16, 9, 2)
Number of errors _____   Time between digits _____   Other _____
Notes _____

$2 + 3 =$ _____ $3 - 2 =$ _____ $4 + 8 =$ _____ $9 + 12 =$ _____
$4 \times 3 =$ _____ $7 \times 4 =$ _____ $12 \times 6 =$ _____ $65 \div 5 =$ _____

Digits forward and backward:
Fwd.   42__   368__   6385__   96725__   864972__   5739481__   31749852__
Bwd.   91__   582__   9147__   63892__   839427__   7392641__   49521863__
Fwd. = ____   Bwd. = ____   Evaluation: __Below average   __ Average   __Above average

D) Memory
Remote Memory
Childhood data: Schools attended_____
                                        Teachers' names/faces _____
                                        Street grew up on _____
                                        Mother's maiden name_____

Significant historical events (e.g., Kennedy's death, Challenger tragedy, Reagan shot) _____
_____

Recent Memory
Activities past few months _____
Past few days _____
Yesterday (events, meals, etc.) _____
Today (events, meals, etc.) _____

30-MINUTE MEMORY CHECK _____

E) Information (knowledge of current events)

Does the client   ___read newspaper?   How often? _____

                   ___TV/radio news?   How often? _____

Name current local/national news _____

President's name _____   Three large cities_____

F) Judgment

"First one in theater to see smoke and fire" _____

"Find stamped envelope in street" _____

G) Abstractive Capacity

PROVERBS   INTERPRETATION GIVEN

"Rolling stone gathers no moss" _____

"Early bird catches the worm" _____

"Strike while the iron is hot" _____

Abstract vs. concrete interpretations _____

H) Insight (awareness of issues; what level?)

__Complete denial   __Slight awareness   __Awareness, but blames others

__Intellectual insight, but few changes likely   __Emotional insight, understanding, changes can occur

Comment on client's level of insight to problems: _____

_____

I) Intellectual level/Education/IQ estimate

Grade in school _____   Ever repeat a grade? ____   Grades/Progress _____

Special education classes _____

Intelligence _____

General knowledge _____

Selective nature of Sx _____

Observations (pain, fatigue, gait, dizziness) _____

Comments _____

J) Adverse Factors Affecting the Child's Ability to Function

(e.g., pain, side effects of meds, dysfunctional family, abuse, physical impairments, etc.)

_____

_____

_____

_____

_____

_____

_____

_____

6) TESTING RESULTS

_____
_____
_____
_____
_____
_____
_____
_____
_____
_____
_____
_____
_____

7) ASSESSMENT

Summary and diagnostic findings (Tie together history and mental status findings and relate to diagnosis. Include onset of current Sx of the condition and how far back it goes. Include prognosis.)

_____
_____
_____
_____
_____
_____
_____
_____
_____
_____
_____

Axis I   _____

Axis II   _____

Axis III _____
Axis IV   _____
Axis V   _____

NOTE: FOR SOCIAL SECURITY DO NOT MAKE A STATEMENT AS TO WHETHER
THE CHILD IS DISABLED

3.55

Chapter 4

Treatment Plan Forms and Procedures

Individual Treatment Plans

Effective treatment plans are designed to provide a clear picture of the client's specific treatment needs. Vague intake information leads to vague treatment plans, which lead to vague treatment, which leads to vague outcomes. No one would sign a contract to have a house built which simply stated, "Build house." The blueprints and contract provide specifications regarding time frame, cost, and outcome. The treatment plan is the "blueprint for therapy."

Typical problems in writing treatment plans include making statements that are too vague or generic, not indicative of the assessment, unrealistic, or not assessable, measurable, or observable. Treatment plans must directly correspond to the assessment material (e.g., purpose, impairments, diagnosis, goals). The treatment plan is driven or documented by the assessment. It must clearly reflect a plan to alleviate impairments resulting from the mental disorder. Regulating sources such as Medicare and the Joint Commission on Accreditation of Healthcare Organizations and most third-party payers require that treatment plans provide measurable outcomes written in behavioral, objective, or measurable terms.

The process of writing a treatment plan begins with an accurate and specific assessment of the client's concerns. Assessment sources include the clinical interview, testing, observations, historical documents, and collateral information.

The plan should reflect both the client's presenting problem and the client's stated needs and goals, and it should also reflect the clinical judgment of the therapist. Both Medicare and Joint Commission guidelines call for specific measurable treatment outcomes to be attained by the client, not the therapist.

Treatment Plan Formats

Treatment plan formats vary, but the required information is fairly consistent. A three-column format (Symptoms, Goals/Objectives, and Treatment Strategies) will be used for examples in this book.

COLUMN ONE, "SYMPTOMS." The first column identifies specific problem areas to be addressed in treatment. The stated symptoms must correspond to, and therefore validate, the client's diagnosis and impairments. Symptoms are not vague terms or constructs such as "depression," but rather symptoms of depression that are causing functional impairment. The symptoms listed must validate and be indicative of the Axis I diagnosis.

The listed symptoms, in themselves, should clearly define the diagnosis. If not, then the diagnosis is not clearly being treated. Some mental health professionals update treatment plans regularly (e.g., every 60 days); in such cases it is obviously not possible to address every symptom of a diagnosis. But nevertheless the symptoms addressed should be indicative of the diagnosis. Prolonged treatment of other diagnoses is not justified unless other diagnoses have been given.

Ethical concerns are noted when practitioners bill insurance companies under one diagnosis but treat a different diagnosis. Potential consequences could range from services not being covered to ethical charges.

COLUMN TWO, "GOALS/OBJECTIVES." The second column lists the client's intended outcomes of treatment, written in measurable, observable, and documentable terms in which the effectiveness of the treatment can be evaluated.

Both goals and objectives are to be listed for each symptom. Goals are defined as overall, global, long-term outcomes. Goals are often the opposite of the symptoms. For example, the goal for a depressed person might be to alleviate depression. It is difficult to measure goals, but they can be broken down into objectives which are observable. Objectives are defined as incremental steps by which goals are attained. They reflect specific improvements in adaptive behaviors resulting in reduction of symptoms. Objectives are revised throughout the course of therapy depending on progress and/or setbacks.

Objectives may be measured in a variety of ways, including successive testing, charting, subjective ratings by the client and/or others, and clinical observations. It is often difficult to write all objectives in measurable, observable, or quantifiable terms, but efforts should be taken to establish a baseline and objective points of comparison. Terms such as "increase" or "decrease" should be clarified with specific quantifiers and qualifiers. For example, an objective of "increase pleasurable social activities to four per week by October 13th" is much more specific and measurable than "increase pleasurable social activities." In the latter example, *any* increase (e.g., .0001 percent) would appear as progress. Specific treatment planning keeps therapy on course. Goals and objectives must be clear in order to be followed.

COLUMN THREE, "STRATEGIES." The third column describes treatment interventions in and out of the sessions by which the treatment goals and objectives will be addressed. Treatment strategies may include the type of therapy (e.g., group, family, individual), school of thought (e.g., cognitive, behavioral, psychoanalytic, Rational Emotive Therapy [RET]), therapeutic techniques (e.g., dream analysis, confrontation, systematic desensitization, role playing), and homework assignments.

Each aspect of the treatment plan requires client collaboration. The client must not only agree on the symptoms, goals and treatment strategies, he or she must also be willing to submit to their integrative process in therapy. The question, "What does the client want to get out of therapy?" is too often ignored. Client/therapist cooperation and collaboration go hand in hand.

Objectives should be written in small, attainable steps. For example, if a socially withdrawn person has a treatment plan objective of initiating five social interactions per week, the likelihood of success may be quite small. But since incremental increases in objective criteria are viewed as more attainable by the client, an initial objective in this case might be to initiate one social interaction per week. The high likelihood of success is in itself rewarding. As an objective is met, new objective criteria are set, up to the point at which impairment is alleviated. Treatment plans are meant to be revised as progress and/or setbacks take place.

Success of a treatment plan also depends on how realistic and achievable the goals are. For example, a treatment plan goal to "eliminate depression" can never be reached since depression is a normal and adaptive human emotion.

Client effort and motivation to fulfill treatment plan objectives merit close attention. The relationship between performance and motivation is curvilinear. That is, low levels or drive lead to low performance because little effort and low reinforcement are perceived. Likewise, high levels of drive generally lead to high levels of anxiety about performance, and thus performance is also low. For example, if a client is suffering from agoraphobia, an objective of going to a shopping mall during the week before Christmas would probably be too anxiety-provoking for any positive performance results. But if the objective is set too low, there might be little or no motivation to change behavior. A moderate amount of drive leads to optimal performance. Discussing specific goals and objectives with the client can certainly help determine the success of a treatment plan and subsequent treatment.

Example of a Poor Treatment Plan

In the example of vague treatment plan statements on page 4.7, entries are neither descriptive, observable, measurable, nor client-specific with respect to functional impairments. No target dates are set. Goals are not broken down into objectives. It is not signed by the client or therapist.

Individual Treatment Plan

CLIENT'S NAME: JD

DATE:

SYMPTOMS	GOALS/OBJECTIVES	TREATMENT STRATEGY
Depression	Eliminate depression	Individual therapy and Prozac
Irritability	Stop mood swings	Therapy
Sadness	Increase outlook	Counseling
Conduct	Stop negative behaviors	Discuss feelings
Anger	Anger management	Listen to tapes
Budgeting	Balance budget	Marriage counseling
Marital discord	Communication skills	Talk therapy

_____

Therapist's Signature

COMPLETED EXAMPLE OF A POOR TREATMENT PLAN

Example of a Good Treatment Plan

Judy Doe

Judy Doe's treatment plan (on page 4.9) is the culmination of the presenting problem, testing, intake questions, clinical observations, and biographical information. During the second session, she and the therapist collaboratively set a course of treatment that met both the professional abilities of the therapist and the therapeutic wants and needs of the client.

The concerns noted in column 1 of the treatment plan serve a variety of functions. First, they validate the diagnosis. Her diagnosis of major depression is validated in her treatment plan for each of the following concerns:

1. Decreased energy level

2. Low ego strength

3. Difficulty concentrating

4. Hopelessness feelings

5. Diminished pleasure

6. Social withdrawal

The goals and objectives are based on, first, alleviation of the symptoms noted in Column 1, and second, on agreed-upon outcomes for Judy Doe to work on in a given time frame. Since not all mental health professionals are competent to treat all clients' concerns, the treatment strategies include referrals to other professionals when necessary. Judy Doe is to receive talk therapy from the psychologist but is referred to her physician for medication and to monitor a physical exercise program.

In this case, the psychologist's training does not permit her to prescribe medications or monitor physical procedures; therefore, a referral is given in these areas. Serious ethical violations may occur when mental health professionals practice outside of their competencies. For example, if a mental health professional were to suggest, or even monitor, a diet or exercise program and the client developed physical problems related to the program, the practitioner could be subject to litigation and possible license revocation.

Individual Treatment Plan

Name: *Doe, Judy* DOB: *7-6-48* Date: *3-15-97*
Presenting Problem: *Depressed mood, irritability* Therapist: *DLB*
Axis I: *296.32 Major depression, recurrent, moderate* Axis II: *Deferred*

Services Needed TREATMENT	Anticipated Number of Sessions							
	0	1	2	3–5	6–10	11–20	21–40	40+
● Assessment	0	0	●	0	0	0	0	0
● Individual	0	0	0	0	0	●	0	0
0 Group	0	0	0	0	0	0	0	0
0 Family	0	0	0	0	0	0	0	0
0 Other	0	0	0	0	0	0	0	0

SYMPTOMS	GOALS/Objectives	TREATMENT STRATEGIES
DEPRESSED MOOD Address following symptoms:	DEVELOP PLAN TO ALLEVIATE EMOTIONAL, OCCUPATIONAL, AND SOCIAL IMPAIRMENT DUE TO DEPRESSED MOOD. RETURN TO PREVIOUS FUNCTIONING LEVELS.	Individual therapy (cognitive-behavioral). Med referral. Possible marital therapy. Successive BDI's. Charting.
1) Decreased energy level	INCREASE ENERGY LEVEL Participate in appropriate physical exercise daily.	Medical evaluation referral. Physical program approved by physician.
2) Low ego strength	INCREASE EGO STRENGTH Accomplish at least one weekly homework assignment which leads to positive outcomes. Log at least one positive self-statement daily. Verbalize awareness of negative self-beliefs.	Focus on positive qualities. Chart and reinforce progress. Role playing. Logging. Experiencing and sharing feelings in session.
3) Difficulty concentrating	IMPROVE ABILITY TO FOCUS ON THOUGHTS/ACTIVITIES Complete an appropriate lesson plan in 45–60 minutes (as per previous functioning).	Learn strategies to break problems down into components.
4) Hopelessness feelings	RESTRUCTURE DYSFUNCTIONAL THOUGHT PROCESSES Chart one future plan daily. Develop insight as to relationship between stressors, anger, and depression.	Analyze dysfunctional thoughts. Keep dysfunctional thought record. Positive outcomes homework.
5) Diminished pleasure	INCREASE PLEASURE IN DAILY ACTIVITIES Increase/maintain selected pleasurable activities to 3X/week.	Incorporate effective time management of pleasurable vs. nonpleasurable activities. Chart and reinforce progress.
6) Social withdrawal	INCREASE SOCIAL INTERACTIONS Increase and maintain at least 2 new social interactions/week.	Role playing. Psychoeducational training. Chart and reinforce progress.

I have discussed the information listed above, various treatment strategies, and their possible outcomes. I have received and/or read my copy of my rights as a client and procedures for reporting grievances. I concur with the above diagnosis and treatment plan.

Judy Doe	*3-15-97*		
Client's Signature	Date	Guardian's Signature	Date
Darlene L. Benton, Ph.D.	*3-15-97*	*Sharon Bell, Ph.D.*	*3-16-97*
Therapist's Signature	Date	Clinical Supervisor	Date

Example of a Child's Treatment Plan

A treatment plan for children is shown on page 4.11. It differs from an adult treatment plan in that the initial sessions are not direct therapy; rather, the initial objectives are to establish a therapeutic relationship, acclimate the child to therapy, and establish rapport and trust. Without these initial sessions the prognosis would be poor.

Individual Treatment Plan—Child

Name: *Rentschler, Johnny* DOB: *3-6-91* Date: *1-29-97*
Presenting Problem: *Anger management, coping, withdrawal* Therapist: *DLB*
Axis I: *Adjustment reaction/depressed mood and conduct* Axis II:

Services Needed TREATMENT	Anticipated Number of Sessions							
	0	1	2	3–5	6–10	11–20	21–40	40+
❂ Assessment	0	0	❂	0	0	0	0	0
❂ Individual	0	0	0	0	0	❂	0	0
0 Group	0	0	0	0	0	0	0	0
❂ Family	0	0	0	0	❂	0	0	0
0 Other	0	0	0	0	0	0	0	0

SYMPTOMS	GOALS/Objectives	TREATMENT STRATEGIES
BEHAVIORAL AND AFFECTIVE DYSFUNCTIONING SINCE RECENT DIVORCE OF PARENTS	*DEVELOP PLAN TO ALLEVIATE EMOTIONAL, BEHAVIORAL, AND SOCIAL IMPAIRMENT, AND INCREASE COPING SKILLS*	*Individual play therapy* *Collateral sessions with mother* *Charting*
INITIAL CONCERNS *1) Lack of trust*	*INCREASE LEVEL OF TRUST* *Develop nonthreatening therapeutic relationship* *ENGAGE IN PLAY THERAPY* *Enactment of psychological conflicts in therapy session*	*Initial sessions incorporating drawings (e.g., draw pictures of family as an expression of affect and to help become comfortable in therapeutic setting).* *Increasing use of play therapy and rapport- and trust-building strategies*
SYMPTOMS *2) Anger/behavioral management* *• Recurrent outbursts toward mother* *• Property damage in the home* *• Bullying/hitting younger sister*	*INCREASE ABILITY TO EXPRESS, CLARIFY, AND LABEL ANGER FEELINGS POSITIVELY* *Current: 4–5 daily outbursts toward family* *3-month objective: 0–2 daily outbursts* *Current: 0 interactions discussing feelings* *3-month objective: discuss, label feelings 1/day*	*Play therapy utilizing safe expression of hostility. Role playing means of appropriately verbalizing related feelings. Charting at home with selective reinforcers such as verbal praise.*
3) Difficulties coping with changes in environment, resulting in increased stress levels	*LEARN SOCIALLY ACCEPTABLE MEANS OF COPING WITH LOSS AND RESULTANT ANGER MANAGEMENT ISSUES*	*Play therapy* *Psychoeducation* *Role playing*
4) Social withdrawal	*INCREASE TIME SPENT WITH SIGNIFICANT OTHERS, ACTIVITIES, AND RECREATION* *Current hours in above activities: 4/week* *3-month objective: 20/week*	*Family assignments encouraging positive social activities* *Charting*

I have discussed the information listed above, various treatment strategies, and their possible outcomes. I have received and/or read my copy of my rights as a client and procedures for reporting grievances. I concur with the above diagnosis and treatment plan.

		Linda Rentschler	*1-29-97*
Client's Signature	Date	Guardian's Signature	Date
Darlene L. Benton, Ph.D.	*1-29-97*	*Sharon Bell, Ph.D.*	*2-3-97*
Therapist's Signature	Date	Clinical Supervisor	Date

Individual Treatment Plan

Name: DOB: Date:
Presenting Problem: Therapist:
Axis I: Axis II:

Services Needed TREATMENT	Anticipated Number of Sessions							
	0	1	2	3–5	6–10	11–20	21–40	40+
0 Assessment	0	0	0	0	0	0	0	0
0 Individual	0	0	0	0	0	0	0	0
0 Group	0	0	0	0	0	0	0	0
0 Family	0	0	0	0	0	0	0	0
0 Other	0	0	0	0	0	0	0	0

SYMPTOMS	GOALS/Objectives	TREATMENT STRATEGIES

I have discussed the information listed above, various treatment strategies, and their possible outcomes. I have received and/or read my copy of my rights as a client and procedures for reporting grievances. I concur with the above diagnosis and treatment plan.

_____   _____   _____   _____
Client's Signature   Date   Guardian's Signature   Date

_____   _____   _____   _____
Therapist's Signature   Date   Clinical Supervisor   Date

Example of a Short-Term Therapy Treatment Plan

The form on page 4.14 depicts a sample treatment plan for short-term therapy in which session content is preplanned according to treatment goals and objectives. It differs from the traditional treatment plans in this book in that it outlines in advance the objectives for each session. Therapy is defined by a set number of sessions in which the focus of each is planned in the initial sessions.

Individual Treatment Plan—Short-Term Therapy

Name: *Roe, Sheila*   DOB: *6-4-58*   Date: *5-7-97*

Presenting Problem: *Depressed mood, irritability*   Therapist: *PS*

AXIS I: *300.4 Dysthymic Disorder*   Axis II: *Deferred*

Services Needed
Anticipated Number of Sessions

TREATMENT	0	1	2	3–5	6–10	11–20	21–40	40+
● Assessment	0	●	0	0	0	0	0	0
● Individual	0	0	0	0	●	0	0	0
0 Group	0	0	0	0	0	0	0	0
0 Family	0	0	0	0	0	0	0	0
0 Other	0	0	0	0	0	0	0	0

SYMPTOMS	GOALS/Objectives	TREATMENT STRATEGIES
DEPRESSED MOOD *Address following symptoms:*	*DEVELOP PLAN TO ALLEVIATE EMOTIONAL, OCCUPATIONAL, AND SOCIAL IMPAIRMENT DUE TO DEPRESSED MOOD.*	*Individual therapy (cognitive-behavioral).* *Possible marital therapy.* *Successive BDIs.*
1) Decreased energy level	*INCREASE ENERGY LEVEL.* *Participate in increased physical activities.*	*Medical evaluation referral.* *Discuss exercise program (M.D. approval).*
2) Hopelessness feelings	*RESTRUCTURE THOUGHTS TO VIEW FUTURE MORE POSITIVELY.* *Chart one future plan daily.*	*Analyze dysfunctional thoughts.* *Keep dysfunctional thought record.* *Positive outcomes homework.*
3) Diminished pleasure	*INCREASE PLEASURE IN DAILY ACTIVITIES* *Increase/maintain selected pleasurable activities to 3x/week.*	*Incorporate effective time management of pleasurable vs. nonpleasurable activities.* *Chart progress.*
4) Social withdrawal	*INCREASE SOCIAL INTERACTIONS.* *Increase/maintain at least 2 new social interactions per week.*	*Role playing.* *Psychoeducational training.* *Chart progress.*

	Sessions (s)	Topic(s)	Sessions (s)	Topic(s)
	1	*Assessment*	*5–6*	*Social withdrawal*
SCHEDULE	*2*	*Treatment planning*		*Diminished pleasure*
OF TOPICS	*3*	*Diminished pleasure*	*7*	*Review progress*
	4	*Hopelessness feelings*	*8–9*	*Hopelessness feelings*
		Diminished pleasure		*Social withdrawal*
			10	*Closure*

I have discussed the information listed above, various treatment strategies, and their possible outcomes. I have received and/or read my copy of my rights as a client and procedures for reporting grievances. I concur with the above diagnosis and treatment plan.

Sheila Roe	*5-7-97*		
Client's Signature	Date	Guardian's Signature	Date
Phillip Schultz, M.S.W.	*5-7-97*	*Sharon Bell, Ph.D.*	*5-7-97*
Therapist's Signature	Date	Clinical Supervisor	Date

Individual Treatment Plan—Short-Term Therapy

Name:				DOB:		Date:	
Presenting Problem:						Therapist:	
Axis I:				Axis II:			

Services Needed	Anticipated Number of Sessions							
TREATMENT	0	1	2	3–5	6–10	11–20	21–40	40+
0 Assessment	0	0	0	0	0	0	0	0
0 Individual	0	0	0	0	0	0	0	0
0 Group	0	0	0	0	0	0	0	0
0 Family	0	0	0	0	0	0	0	0
0 Other	0	0	0	0	0	0	0	0

SYMPTOMS	GOALS/Objectives	TREATMENT STRATEGIES

	Sessions (s)	Topic(s)		Sessions (s)	Topic(s)
SCHEDULE OF TOPICS					

I have discussed the information listed above, various treatment strategies, and their possible outcomes. I have received and/or read my copy of my rights as a client and procedures for reporting grievances. I concur with the above diagnosis and treatment plan.

_____   _____   _____   _____
Client's Signature   Date   Guardian's Signature   Date

_____   _____   _____   _____
Therapist's Signature   Date   Clinical Supervisor   Date

Chapter 5

Case Notes and Prior Authorization Request Forms and Procedures

In-Session Case Notes

Case notes are designed to document the course of therapy. They should clearly reflect the implementation of the treatment plan and assessment. The treatment plan symptoms, objectives, and treatment strategies must be documented regularly in the case notes.

Various formats for writing case notes such as DAP and SOAP are commonly used. Organized case notes provide structure to case note writing, rather than simply summarizing a session. The acronym DAP stands for data, assessment, and plan. SOAP stands for subjective, objective, assessment, and plan. The DAP format will be used for examples in this book.

Data

The Data section of the case notes is oriented to address a number of clinical concerns or questions. Although the case notes may not specifically cover each of the following areas of documentation, overall they should reflect:

What specifically took place in the session

Therapeutic interventions

Clinical observations

Test results

Homework assignments

Current documentation of the diagnosis

Current stressors, impairments, and affective and cognitive concerns

Current behavioral concerns

As in the scientific method, data provides information by which to assess a client's current condition, assess the progress of therapy, and plan upcoming interventions based on current data and assessment. Specifically, documentation in the Data section includes the following.

CLINICAL DIAGNOSIS. An outside reader should be able to determine the diagnosis, current issues, treatment, and interventions by the content of the case notes. For example, if the diagnosis is an adjustment disorder, the case notes should document an adjustment disorder by addressing the current stressor(s) and the resulting affective/behavioral issues noted in the diagnosis. Likewise, if the diagnosis is a conduct disorder, case notes should clearly address treatment of conduct, not depression, unless there is a secondary diagnosis of depression. Of course, secondary issues may be documented and noted, but case notes must be consistent with the primary diagnosis and treatment objectives of the session.

FUNCTIONAL IMPAIRMENTS. Medical necessity of treatment is defined as "significant impairment or dysfunction as a result of a mental disorder." Symptoms and impairments differ in that symptoms help define the DSM-IV diagnosis, but do not adequately specify which areas of the client's life are adversely affected. The specific ways in which symptoms adversely affect the client's life are referred to as impairments. The course of treatment is aimed at alleviating the functional impairments resulting from the DSM symptoms of the diagnosis. As treatment progresses, functional impairments decrease. Regular charting of ongoing functional impairments is crucial to documentation of the course of treatment. When functional impairments no longer validate or justify a diagnosis, most third-party payers no longer cover services. But if case notes do not validate functional impairments, there is no "documented behavioral evidence"; thus an audit or case review could result in funds paid for services being returned. As the treatment is revised, it addresses current functional impairments.

Types of functional impairments include social, family, occupational, affective, physical, cognitive, sexual, educational, biopsychological, and other areas in life that could lead to dysfunction. Documentation of functional impairments includes providing specific examples that are measurable. For example, a client with major depression might be impaired occupationally by significant decreases in work production; thus his or her job future might be in jeopardy. Documentation could include comparisons of previous functioning (e.g., producing 10 widgets per week) to current functioning (e.g., producing 3 widgets per week due to fatigue, low motivation, missing work, etc.). Case notes could document specific interventions to alleviate fatigue, low motivation, and missing work, and subsequently document the resulting production at work. Charting such as shown in Figure 5.1 could aid the documentation. The goal of such documentation is not to produce a graph, but rather to provide evidence of progress or setbacks in order to monitor and document therapeutic effectiveness of therapy and client participation.

TREATMENT PLAN SYMPTOMS, GOALS, AND OBJECTIVES. The documentation of clinical symptoms is similar to that of functional impairments. In the previous example, a functional impairment

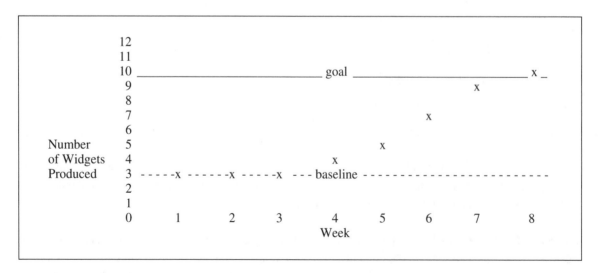

Figure 5.1 Graph Charting Patient Progress Based on Effectiveness of Therapy.

was less production at work, while symptoms included fatigue, low motivation, and missing work. Documentation of symptoms includes noting ongoing frequency, duration, and intensity of symptoms. Charting techniques may be employed, and may include simple notation in the chart for later comparisons. Each therapeutic session has specific objectives taken directly from the treatment plan.

THERAPEUTIC INTERVENTIONS. Documentation of clinical interventions is required in case notes. Charting statements both reflect and document accepted therapeutic interventions. Most third-party payers require that the techniques employed in therapy are not experimental in nature. Notes should reflect specific techniques, interventions, and their outcomes. Such information will provide an empirical rationale to continue, discontinue, or modify the specific course of therapy. Intervention statements also include evaluation of client homework assignments prescribed in therapy.

CURRENT ISSUES/STRESSORS. Case notes should provide ongoing evidence of current stressors and problems, as well as positive aspects in the client's life. Documented therapeutic interventions are directed at alleviating impairments resulting from these stressors. Therapeutic techniques are noted that document interventions designed to cope with current issues and stressors. Ongoing documentation assesses therapeutic results.

OBSERVATIONS. Clinical observations written in the case notes provide ongoing statements in areas such as affect, mental status, contact with reality, nonverbal behaviors, unusual behaviors or statements, contradictory statements, and so forth that provide additional documentation of the need for services. Examples of affective observations include psychomotor retardation/agitation and level of affect (e.g., normal, restricted, blunted, or flat). Other examples may be found on pages 2.55 and 2.56 in the Mental Status Exam section of the Diagnostic Assessment Report and in the Diagnostic Interview Form. Several publications are available describing such terminology (see Bibliography).

Assessment

The Assessment section of the case notes is used for evaluation of the course of therapy based on the most recent data (results of the current session). Assessment may include the current session and a cumulative assessment of the therapy in general. The following areas may be evaluated:

The session

The course of therapy

Client cooperation/insight/motivation

Client progress/setbacks

Areas needing more work

Impairments

Treatment strategies

How treatment plan objectives are being met

Changes needed to stay on target

Plan

The Plan section of the case notes is based on the Assessment. The question asked is, "Based on the current assessment, what will be done to most effectively meet the treatment plan objectives?" A confirmation and/or revision of the treatment plan, this section may include plans for:

Homework assignments

Upcoming interventions

The next session or series of sessions

Treatment plan revisions in objectives or strategies

Common Errors in Case Notes

The form on page 5.9 illustrates several common errors.

Errors of Omission

1. No date (M/D/Y)

2. No stated objectives for the session. The content of the session should follow specific treatment plan objectives and be documented in the case notes.

3. No signature of therapist. Initials are not sufficient.

4. No start and ending time. Notations such as "1 hr" are often not sufficient for documentation unless exact times are documented in a ledger or date book.

Errors of Commission. Each case note statement is quite vague and does not validate any diagnosis or impairments.

5. "Did his homework."

   Although this statement may suggest client compliance, it does not provide information on the therapeutic effectiveness of the activity or suggest how it meets treatment plan objectives. Homework assignments should be documented concerning their therapeutic effectiveness and should be consistent with accepted procedures in the mental health field.

6. "Took test."

   Ongoing testing is certainly an effective means of documentation, but the specific test given and the results are needed to provide data for reference. It is possible to chart results of ongoing testing. A brief interpretation is also suggested.

7. "Talked about. . . . Went over. . . . Discussed. . . ."

   Statements such as these indicate to some degree the content of the session, but provide no indication of how the treatment plan is being followed or documented.

8. There should be no open spaces left where additional information could later be added to the case notes. Lines should fill up this space to prevent fabricating information after the fact. When a therapist recalls information at a later date, it should be written as an addendum, rather than simply penciled in.

9. "Waive co-payment. . . ."
   Such procedures are illegal and constitute insurance fraud.

Case Notes

Name: *John* **Date:** *Monday*

John was on time for his appointment. Did his homework. Took test.
Talked about his homework. Went over marital relationship. Discussed
events of week and how they relate to counseling. Was happy about talking
to his uncle on the phone.

Went over homework and made plans. Worked on communication skills.
Positive communication is important. Will come again.

(Note: waive co-payment if insurance pays their portion)

_____
Therapist's Signature

EXAMPLE OF COMPLETED POOR CASE NOTES

Saving Time in
Case Note Writing

Approximately 75 percent of the therapists surveyed by this author have indicated that they write case notes after the session (see pages 5.12 and 5.13). They believe that if they took case notes during the session they would not be able to attend to the client as well and that writing case notes after the session helps to provide an overall picture of the session.

However, other therapists have stated that their case note details and accuracy have increased when they started writing the notes during the session. They add that the transition often takes a few months. The form on page 5.15 entitled Case Notes—Outline can be used during the transition from taking case notes after the session to taking them during the session.

In some cases writing case notes during the session can increase rapport and empathy. When the therapist nonverbally portrays the message, "What you say is important, so I must write it down," case note writing during the session can be both time-saving and therapeutic.

Sample Case Notes

Two sample case notes are included. The first, on page 5.12, is for an adult client named John Doe and is designed to document evidence of the course of therapy and follow the DAP guidelines discussed previously. The second, on page 5.13, is for a child. It follows the treatment plan from page 4.11.

Case Notes—Adult

Client: John Doe   **Session:** 5   **Date:** 2-13-97
Diagnosis: 300.4 Dysthymia
Tx Goals: Ego strength/Positive thoughts   **Therapist:** PS

D Completed homework assignment of identifying dysfunctional thoughts. Reviewed five positive qualities and five perceived negative characteristics from previous session. Several self-depracating statements. Current BDI score = 28 (previous week = 32). Difficulties believing that he is capable of being happy. Describes self as being easily irritated and less capable than most other people. Fairly upset about continued spousal discord. Two divorce threats this week. Now sleeping in guest room; angry, frustrated, sad. States much guilt and remorse over his irritability, which he believes causes others to reject him. Charted progress of social contacts. Continues to meet current homework goals of one new social interaction per week. Describes affective level past week as sad about 50% of the time. (Charting indicates previous four weeks = 60–75% of time feeling sad.) Missed one day at work this week due to feelings of boredom/fatigue. <u>Sessions Topics: Ego strength.</u> Role-played speaking with assertiveness to spouse, employer, and in job interview. <u>Positive thoughts.</u> States no positive plan or goals for future. History of others making his decisions (parents, relatives, spouse). Identified three attainable short-term goals that he is interested in pursuing: 1) enrolling in community education course or seminar, 2) weekend trip, 3) volunteering at nursing home once per week. ——————

A Increased focus on personal responsibility for behavioral/affective change and in self-direction. Viewing self more positively in past few weeks. Continued concerns with level of irritability and spousal discord. Progress in individual concerns, but low motivation in spousal issues and missing work. Compliant in homework assignments, but level of insight moderately low. Behavioral techniques seem most helpful. ——————

P Homework: Implement one of three above listed short-term goals. Continue dysfunctional thought record. Client is considering spousal involvement in therapy in 3–4 weeks. ——————

Time Started: 4:00 p.m.   **Time Finished:** 4:51 p.m.   **Duration:** 1 hour
Next Appointment: Date: 2-20-97   **Time:** 2:00 p.m.

Therapist's Signature Phillip Schultz, M.S.W.

Case Notes—Child

Client: _Johnny Rentschler_   **Session:** _3_   **Date:** _2-12-97_

Diagnosis: _Adjustment reaction with depressed mood/conduct_

Tx Goals: _Establish trust/Engage in play therapy_   **Therapist:** _SB_

(D) 1st session since assessment. <u>Mother present.</u> Began session with mother bringing in chart of 38 physical aggressions in past week directed toward people, and 12 incidents of property damage in the home. Major aggression toward sister after two attempts by Johnny to phone father who did not return phone calls. Mother further noted receiving two notes from teacher describing initiating fights in school. Possible suspension impending. Mother further notes that Johnny refused to go on family outing to visit friends in old neighborhood. Spent most of weekend in his room watching TV and playing video games. Refused to play with same-aged cousin, whom mother invited to home. Loaned mother copy of "Parental Consistency Manual."
<u>Mother not present.</u> Asked Johnny to draw portrait of his family. Quickly drew colorful picture with all family members in a boxing ring. Everyone in the family except Johnny had hands tied. Mother was kicking at him. He was the only one able to fight with his hands. (See drawing dated 2-12-95.) Note father's placement on other side of ropes in opposite corner. When invited to discuss the drawing, Johnny stated that dad is far away and can't be reached because his mother is in the way and his sister is on his mother's side. He further noted that his mother and sister can not hurt him, like his father did before, or they will also get in trouble.

(A) Much blaming of mother for father's absence. Resentment and anger toward family, whom he views as responsible for father now being unapproachable. Deep sense of loss. Seems to view family as choosing sides against him, but they are unable to control his behaviors without getting into legal trouble. Views situation as having few available options to cope with perceived rejection. Insight into source of anger slowly developing. Views control as rewarding.

(P) "Functional Analysis of Behavior" form to be completed by mother. Continue with drawings in which he draws/discusses changes he desires and related affect. Continue nonthreatening enactments of family dynamics. Continue rapport/trust building.

Time Started: _2:00 p.m._   **Time Finished:** _2:49 p.m._   **Duration:** _1 hour_

Next Appointment: Date: _2-19-97_   **Time:** _2:00 p.m._

Therapist's Signature _Sharon Bell, Ph.D._

Case Notes—Outline

This form provides structure and reminders to the therapist as to what areas of documentation are helpful in case notes. Although the information contained in the case notes is the same as previous examples, this form breaks down the DAP format into specific content areas. The form is not designed to model a particular type of treatment, but rather to provide evidence of on-target treatment for any therapeutic stance.

Some therapists using this form prefer to jot brief notes during the session to be used as reminders when they write the final copy of their case notes. Others use this form as a final product. This form can also serve as a transition for therapists in the process of changing their procedure from writing case notes after the session to writing them during the session.

Judy Doe

A Case Note—Outline form for Judy Doe's third session in therapy is provided on page 5.15. The DAP format is used, but the specific documentation needed for each section is addressed.

Case Notes—Outline

Name: _Judy Doe_   Therapist: _DLB_   Date: _3-22-97_

Axis I: _296.32 Major depression, recurrent, moderate_   Axis II: _Deferred_

Session Goals/Objectives _Hopelessness: Restructure dysfunctional thoughts_

DATA

Homework from Past Session(s) _Completed homework assigned; identified uncomfortable situations leading to depression and hopelessness._

Functional Impairment (e.g., emotional, social, occupational, legal, behavioral; include degree, frequency.

duration) _Poor appetite. One meal/day, increasing fatigue. Little social support at home. Very little time spent with spouse or children this week, no sexual desire in 2–3 months. Continues usually feeling depressed, guilty, and angry. Low motivation to teach students. Missed one day of work; no energy, motivation._

Current Issues/Topics/Stressors _Angry because both students and her family will not become motivated to her expectations. States it is her fault. Increasing anger toward spouse due to not supporting her parenting decisions. Much self-blame for others not performing. Notes guilt feelings if she does not chauffeur her children like "other parents."_

Interventions _Discussed and identified 3 dysfunctional thoughts and their respective situations and associated feelings. Vented feelings of anger toward her family and students via empty chair. Confronted defensiveness about accepting others' negative treatment toward her as acceptable._

Observations _Poor eye contact, slumped posture, closed body position, monotonous speech, restricted affect. Less psychomotor agitation during periods of insight._

Other _SUDs level of depression = 88. Baseline = 95. See Subjective Units of Distress (SUDs) charts._

ASSESSMENT (Progress/Impairment/Effectiveness of interventions) _Increased insight into relationship between "shoulds" from parents and current affective/behavioral concerns. Differentiating thoughts and feelings is quite helpful. Difficulties accepting that she is angry at others._

PLAN (Homework, Objectives next session, Changes, Testing) _Dysfunctional thought record as homework. Read "Escape from Co-dependency." Next session: Pleasurable activities._

Start _1:00_   End _1:52_   Time _1 hour_   Next Appt. _3-29-97_   @ _1:00_

Darlene L. Benton, Ph.D.

Therapist's Signature

Case Notes

Client: _____ Date: _____

Diagnosis: _____ Treatment Goals: _____

1 _____

2 _____

3 _____

4 _____

5 _____

6 _____

7 _____

8 _____

9 _____

10 _____

11 _____

12 _____

13 _____

14 _____

15 _____

16 _____

17 _____

18 _____

19 _____

20 _____

21 _____

22 _____

23 _____

24 _____

25 _____

Tests/Handouts Given: _____

Time Started: _____ Time Finished: _____ Duration: _____

Therapist's Signature _____ Next Appt: _____

Case Notes—Outline

Name: _____ Therapist: _____ Date: _____

Axis I: _____ Axis II:_____

Session Goals/Objectives _____

DATA Homework from Past Session(s) _____

_____

Functional Impairment (e.g., emotional, social, occupational, legal, behavioral; include degree, frequency.

duration) _____

_____

_____

_____

Current Issues/Topics/Stressors _____

_____

_____

_____

Interventions _____

_____

_____

_____

Observations _____

_____

Other _____

ASSESSMENT (Progress/Impairment/Effectiveness of interventions) _____

_____

_____

_____

PLAN (Homework, Objectives next session, Changes, Testing)_____

_____

Start _____ End _____ Time _____ Next Appt. _____ @ _____

_____
Therapist's Signature

Group Therapy
Case Notes

Few group therapists have time to write separate and concise case notes for an entire group. Some therapists have reported that they spend more time after the session writing case notes than the time spent in the session. Others report that they use the same case note for the entire session, noting contributions for each client. The latter practice poses ethics problems due to confidentiality being broken if any of the group members' files are released to an outside source.

The Group Therapy Case Notes form on page 5.19 is designed to enable the therapist to take separate notes on each group member during the session. Information that is common to all group members (treatment plan objectives for the session) is listed under Group Topics Discussed. Twelve group behaviors are rated in the Group Behavior Ratings section. Over the course of group therapy these ratings can be assessed for various areas of progress. The remaining space on the form allows for Individual Contributions, which may be documented as the client speaks.

The group case note form also includes a periodic summary that is helpful when case notes are regularly forwarded to others such as parents, guardians, social workers, or group homes.

Group Therapy Case Notes

Client ___Pat Anderson___ Group _Grief_ Date _3-10-97_

AGENDA: GROUP TOPICS DISCUSSED
Session 6 Agenda: 1) Expressing grief 2) Coping with changes
Next week: 1) Saying "good-bye" 2) Future plans

GROUP BEHAVIOR RATINGS

	Low		Medium		High
Seemed interested in the group	O	O	●	O	O
Initiated positive interactions	O	●	O	O	O
Shared emotions	O	O	●	O	O
Helpful to others	O	●	O	O	O
Focused on group tasks	O	O	●	O	O
Disclosed information about self	O	O	●	O	O
Understood group topics	O	O	●	O	O
Participated in group exercises	O	O	●	O	O
Showed listening skills/empathy	O	O	O	●	O
Offered opinions/suggestions/feedback	O	O	●	O	O
Seemed to benefit from the session	O	O	●	O	O
Treatment considerations addressed	O	O	O	●	O

MONTHLY EVALUATION
(fill out last group of each month)

TOPIC	PROGRESS		
	Low	Med	High
Participation	0	0	0
Discusses issues	0	0	0
Insight	0	0	0
Motivation	0	0	0
Emotional expression	0	0	0
Stays on task	0	0	0
Objectives being met	0	0	0

SUGGESTIONS
__ Individual counseling
__ Evaluation for meds
__ Other _____

INDIVIDUAL CONTRIBUTIONS THIS SESSION

Pat was 10 minutes late for the session. Did not seem interested in discussing how he is currently handling death of his parents in auto accident. During a group exercise he disclosed that he cries every night before going to sleep and wakes up 3–4 times per night thinking that his parents are in the room. Has not been doing most of his homework in college, but reports slight increases in homework compliance in past 2 weeks. Generally quiet (but seemed to listen/empathize) when other people discussed their coping strategies dealing with loss of loved ones.

___Clara Nielson, L.C.S.W.___
Therapist

___Fred Jorbell, M.A.___
Cotherapist

Time Started ___7:00 p.m.___

Time Finished ___8:30 p.m.___

Duration ___1½ hrs.___

Group Therapy Case Notes

Client _____ Group _____ Date _____

AGENDA: GROUP TOPICS DISCUSSED

_____
_____

GROUP BEHAVIOR RATINGS	Low		Medium		High
Seemed interested in the group	O	O	O	O	O
Initiated positive interactions	O	O	O	O	O
Shared emotions	O	O	O	O	O
Helpful to others	O	O	O	O	O
Focused on group tasks	O	O	O	O	O
Disclosed information about self	O	O	O	O	O
Understood group topics	O	O	O	O	O
Participated in group exercises	O	O	O	O	O
Showed listening skills/empathy	O	O	O	O	O
Offered opinions/suggestions/feedback	O	O	O	O	O
Seemed to benefit from the session	O	O	O	O	O
Treatment considerations addressed	O	O	O	O	O

MONTHLY EVALUATION
(fill out last group of each month)

TOPIC	PROGRESS		
	Low	Med	High
Participation	0	0	0
Discusses issues	0	0	0
Insight	0	0	0
Motivation	0	0	0
Emotional expression	0	0	0
Stays on task	0	0	0
Objectives being met	0	0	0

SUGGESTIONS

__ Individual counseling

__ Evaluation for meds

__ Other _____

INDIVIDUAL CONTRIBUTIONS THIS SESSION

_____
_____
_____
_____
_____
_____
_____
_____

_____

Therapist

_____

Cotherapist

Time Started _____

Time Finished _____

Duration _____

Third-Party Prior Authorization Request for Continued Services

Many third-party payers initially approve fewer than three initial sessions for assessment and then request a prior authorization (PA) for continued services at regular intervals. Every third-party payer has its own form for requesting continued services. Therapists often complain of their requests usually being turned down, causing services to be quickly terminated due to lack of insurance coverage. As a result, cognitive dissonance persists. Often, the true issue is the therapist's lack of training in writing the PA request, rather than the third-party payer's refusal to continue services. Requesting a PA for services requires concise writing skills in which documenting medical necessity is essential.

The forms on pages 5.22 and 5.23 represent PAs from the file of Judy Doe. These samples represent a typical PA format. The first is completed vaguely and does not provide sufficient documentation of diagnosis, symptoms, impairments, therapeutic progress/setbacks, and so on. It is written in a manner suggesting that the client has improved significantly and does not need further services. If this were the case, further services should not be requested. But, if additional mental health services are medically necessary, the documentation provided in this form would be a disservice to the client.

Some therapists have noted that writing a PA request is a "Catch-22" situation. That is, if significant improvements are noted as in this form, the PA will be denied because goals apparently have been met sufficiently. On the other hand, if continued severe impairments are noted, it may appear that treatment is ineffective, so the PA will likewise be denied.

The form on page 5.23 provides specific examples of Judy Doe's progress in therapy and documents a continued need to work on other treatment plan goals. This one-page document attempts to summarize the entire course of treatment. The quantified examples are taken directly from the well-documented case notes, rather than offering a nondocumented opinion at the time of writing the PA request.

Third-Party Prior Authorization Request

(Provider Information)   *Judy Doe*   (Patient Information)

	ICD	or	DSM
Primary Diagnosis _Depression_	_____		_____
Secondary Diagnosis _____	_____		_____

Initial Service Date _____   Dates Requested: From _9-7-97_   through _9-7-98_

Hours used _10_   Type(s) of service(s) and hours requested____*Counseling*____

Describe mental health history and current mental status with documentation of diagnosis.

Has been in counseling several times in life. History of marital issues. Mental status indicates need for counseling. Continues to meet diagnostic criteria for depression.

Current stressors and functional impairment. Include psychological impairment as a result of this disorder.

Marital conflict. Does not like her job. Psychological impairment due to issues relating to people who upset her.

Rating of patient's progress in therapy.   Poor   1   2   3   4   5   ⑥   High
Documentation of progress.

Client is doing very well in therapy. Able to discuss issues which are difficult to discuss with spouse.

Rating of patient's cooperation.   Poor   1   2   3   4   5   ⑥   High
Describe willingness to follow treatment plan.

Always willing to participate in discussions in treatment sessions.

Current medications. Therapists contact with primary care physician.

None needed. No referrals necessary.

Discharge plans. Include objective criteria.

Client agrees to remain in treatment until marriage issues are resolved.

Signature _____   Date _____

EXAMPLE OF
POOR THIRD-PARTY
P.A. REQUEST

5.22

Third-Party Prior Authorization Request

(Provider Information)   *Judy Doe*   (Patient Information)

	ICD	or	DSM

Primary Diagnosis *Major depression, moderate, recurrent* _____ _____ *296.32*

Secondary Diagnosis _____ _____ _____

Initial Service Date *1-27-95*   Dates Requested: From *9-7-95*   through *12-7-97*

Hours used *6*   Type(s) of service(s) and hours requested *Individual psychotherapy—15 hrs*

Describe mental health history and current mental status with documentation of diagnosis.

Hx of mental health; Dx of Major depression since 1976. Three in-patient hospitalizations due to suicidal threats/attempts. Other Tx since 1976 includes 6 months of group therapy, 3 attempts of individual therapy (each <10 sessions), and ongoing med management. Appears depressed/psychomotor retardation/fatigued/low motivation/weight loss of 20# in past 3 months/sleeping 12 hrs/day. Oriented x3. No evidence of thought disorder. Family Hx of depression (Dx, Tx, hospital).

Current stressors and functional impairment. Include psychological impairment as a result of this disorder.

Unemployment due to being fired from job (excessive absences). Few/no friends. Divorced six weeks ago. No immediate family in geographic area. Excessive social withdrawal (spends most of day in home, has refused invitations of former friends to attend social functions). Sad most of time, low motivation. Notes difficulty concentrating when filling out job applications.

Rating of patient's progress in therapy.   Poor 1   2   3   ④   5   6   High

Documentation of progress.

Documentation of Progress. Client notes that she wants to change her outlook on life. Has successfully accomplished two of four homework assignments involving initiating social interactions, time management, and involving herself in pleasurable activities. Increase insight regarding dysfunctional thought processes. Gains in ability to make positive self-statements. Continued concerns in social withdrawal and low motivation. Presently focusing on assertiveness skills.

Rating of patient's cooperation.   Poor 1   2   3   4   5   ⑥   High

Describe willingness to follow treatment plan.

High degree of cooperation, but perhaps due to overdependence. Generally agrees with interpretative statements, but in a seemingly dependent manner. Recent attempts at role playing assertiveness have been facilitative.

Current medications. Therapists contact with primary care physician.

Current meds include Prozac from MD. Noted compliance. Collaborative treatment with MD. Shared Tx plans. Summary of sessions exchanged monthly.

Discharge plans. Include objective criteria.

See attached Tx plan for specific goals to be accomplished during course of therapy including: Consistent BDI score of <15, 8 hrs of sleep per night/5 job applications per week until job is acquired/acceptable subjective rating of level of impairment due to depression. Tapering off of sessions. Current weekly visits will become every other week as of session 10.

  Darlene L. Benton, Ph.D.   *Clinical psychologist*   *8-17-97*

Signature   Professional Title   Date

Chapter 6

Relationship Counseling
Forms and Procedures

Marital and Couple's Information Forms

Although similar in format, the Marital Information Form starting on page 6.4 and the Couple's Information Form starting on page 6.14 differ in the choice of wording in the questions. The marital form refers to the "spouse" and to concerns in the "marriage," while the couple's form addresses the "relationship." Experience has taught that using the same form for married and nonmarried clients may cause complaints.

Each form provides valuable information regarding strengths and weaknesses in the relationship. Each partner's point of view and perspective on their partner's point of view are assessed to help increase clients' understanding of each other. The forms end with a written consent for the therapist to discuss each other's responses.

Marital Information Form

1) Name: _Bobby Chen_   2) Age: _30_   3) Date: _3-12-97_

4) Address: _2345 6th Ave._   _Minneapolis_   _CA_   _00032_
       Street & Number   City   State   Zip

5) Briefly, what is your main purpose in coming to marital therapy?: _Often disagreeing_
over finances and how to raise our children. Often do not talk for several days.

INSTRUCTIONS: To assist us in helping you, please fill out this form as fully and openly as possible. Your answers will help plan a course of marital therapy that is most suitable for you and your spouse. Do not exchange this information with your spouse.

Several of your answers on this form may be shared later with your spouse during joint therapy sessions if you give us permission to share this information. For this reason you are advised to respond honestly and carefully to each item. If certain questions do not apply to you or you do not want to share this information, please leave them blank.

6) Is this your first marriage?: Yes _X_   No _____
   If No, which marriage is it for you?:   2   3   4   5+

7) How long have you and your present spouse been married?: _8 years_

8) Are you and your spouse presently living together?: Yes _X_   No _____
   If No, why not?: _____

9) How many times have you and your spouse separated?: _None_

10) Fill out the following information for each child of whom the natural parent is both you and your partner, children from previous relationships, and adopted children.

*"Whose Child?" answering options: B=Both of ours, natural child
                                       BA=Both of ours, adopted (or taken on)
                                       M=My natural child
                                       MA=My child, adopted (or taken on)
                                       S=Spouse's natural child
                                       SA=Spouse's child, adopted (or taken on)

Child's Name	Age	Sex	*Whose Child?	Lives with You and Spouse?
1) _Sally_	5	(F) M	B	X Yes ___No
2) _David_	3	F (M)	B	X Yes ___No
3) _____	___	F M	_____	___Yes ___No
4) _____	___	F M	_____	___Yes ___No
5) _____	___	F M	_____	___Yes ___No
6) _____	___	F M	_____	___Yes ___No
7) _____	___	F M	_____	___Yes ___No
8) _____	___	F M	_____	___Yes ___No

11) List five qualities that initially
   attracted you to your spouse:

   Does your spouse still possess this trait?

   1) _Intelligent_ — X Yes ___ No
   2) _Pretty_ — X Yes ___ No
   3) _Could talk about differences_ — ___ Yes X No
   4) _Spontaneous_ — ___ Yes X No
   5) _____ — ___ Yes ___ No

12) List four negative concerns that
   you initially had in the relationship:

   Does your spouse still possess this trait?

   1) _Judgmental_ — X Yes ___ No
   2) _Set in her ways_ — X Yes ___ No
   3) _Must be right all the time_ — X Yes ___ No
   4) _____ — ___ Yes ___ No

13) List five present positive
   attributes of your spouse:

   Do you often praise your spouse for this trait?

   1) _Works hard on job_ — ___ Yes X No
   2) _Cares about the children_ — ___ Yes X No
   3) _Manages home finances_ — ___ Yes X No
   4) _Attractive_ — X Yes ___ No
   5) _Intelligent_ — ___ Yes X No

14) List five present negative
   attributes of your spouse:

   Do you nag your spouse about this trait?

   1) _Judgmental_ — X Yes ___ No
   2) _Must be right or keeps on arguing_ — X Yes ___ No
   3) _Silent treatment to me_ — X Yes ___ No
   4) _Flirty to other men_ — X Yes ___ No
   5) _____ — ___ Yes ___ No

15) List five things that you do (or
   could do) to make the marriage
   more fulfilling for your spouse:

   Do you often implement this behavior?

   1) _Listen to her point of view_ — ___ Yes X No
   2) _Thank her for managing the finances_ — ___ Yes X No
   3) _Show appreciation for being a good mother_ — ___ Yes X No
   4) _I could clean up more after myself_ — ___ Yes X No
   5) _____ — ___ Yes ___ No

16) List five things that your spouse
   does (or could do) to make the
   marriage more fulfilling for you:

   Does your spouse often implement this behavior?

   1) _Show me more appreciation_ — ___ Yes X No
   2) _Listen to my opinions about the children and money_ — ___ Yes X No
   3) _Ask for my advice, rather than asking her mother_ — ___ Yes X No
   4) _Sexual spontaneity_ — ___ Yes X No
   5) _____ — ___ Yes ___ No

17) List five expectations or dreams you had about marriage
   before you married your spouse:

   Has this been fulfilled?

   1) _Work as a team with children and money_ — ___ Yes X No
   2) _Spouses should be best friends_ — ___ Yes X No
   3) _If we talk things will work out_ — ___ Yes X No
   4) _Love will conquer all_ — ___ Yes X No
   5) _Raise at least 2 children_ — X Yes ___ No

18) On a scale of 1 to 5 rate the following items as they pertain to:

    1) The present state of the marriage
    2) Your need or desire for it
    3) Your spouse's need or desire for it

CIRCLE THE APPROPRIATE RESPONSE FOR EACH

		Present State of the Marriage Poor ... Great	Your Need or Desire Low ... High	Spouse's Need or Desire Low ... High
1)	Affection	1 ②3 4 5	1 2 3 4 ⑤	1 2 ③4 5
2)	Childrearing rules	①2 3 4 5	1 ②3 4 5	1 2 3 4 ⑤
3)	Commitment together	1 ②3 4 5	1 2 3 ④5	1 2 3 ④5
4)	Communication	1 ②3 4 5	1 2 3 ④5	1 2 3 ④5
5)	Emotional closeness	1 ②3 4 5	1 2 3 ④5	1 2 3 ④5
6)	Financial security	1 2 ③4 5	1 2 ③4 5	1 2 3 4 ⑤
7)	Honesty	1 2 ③4 5	1 2 3 ④5	1 2 3 ④5
8)	Housework sharing	1 ②3 4 5	1 ②3 4 5	1 2 3 4 ⑤
9)	Love	1 2 ③4 5	1 2 3 ④5	1 2 3 4 ⑤
10)	Physical attraction	1 ②3 4 5	1 2 3 4 ⑤	1 2 3 ④5
11)	Religious commitment	1 ②3 4 5	1 ②3 4 5	1 2 3 ④5
12)	Respect	①2 3 4 5	1 2 3 4 ⑤	1 2 3 ④5
13)	Sexual fulfillment	1 ②3 4 5	1 2 3 4 ⑤	1 2 ③4 5
14)	Social life together	1 2 ③4 5	1 2 ③4 5	1 2 ③4 5
15)	Time together	1 ②3 4 5	1 2 3 ④5	1 2 3 4 ⑤
16)	Trust	1 2 ③4 5	1 2 3 ④5	1 2 3 4 ⑤
	Other (specify)			
17)	_____	1 2 3 4 5	1 2 3 4 5	1 2 3 4 5
18)	_____	1 2 3 4 5	1 2 3 4 5	1 2 3 4 5
19)	_____	1 2 3 4 5	1 2 3 4 5	1 2 3 4 5
20)	_____	1 2 3 4 5	1 2 3 4 5	1 2 3 4 5

19) Which partner spends more time conducting the following activities?:

CIRCLE THE APPROPRIATE RESPONSE FOR EACH.
M=Me, **S**=Spouse, **E**=Equal time

		M S E	Is this equitable (fair)?	Comments
1)	Auto repairs	Ⓜ S E	_X_ Yes ____ No	
2)	Child care	M Ⓢ E	____ Yes _X_ No	
3)	Child discipline	M Ⓢ E	____ Yes _X_ No	
4)	Cleaning bathrooms	M Ⓢ E	_X_ Yes ____ No	
5)	Cooking	M Ⓢ E	_X_ Yes ____ No	
6)	Employment	M S Ⓔ	_X_ Yes ____ No	
7)	Grocery shopping	M S Ⓔ	_X_ Yes ____ No	
8)	House cleaning	M Ⓢ E	____ Yes _X_ No	
9)	Inside repairs	Ⓜ S E	_X_ Yes ____ No	
10)	Laundry	M Ⓢ E	_X_ Yes ____ No	
11)	Making bed	M S Ⓔ	_X_ Yes ____ No	
12)	Outside repairs	Ⓜ S E	_X_ Yes ____ No	
13)	Recreational events	Ⓜ S E	_X_ Yes ____ No	
14)	Social activities	M S Ⓔ	_X_ Yes ____ No	
15)	Sweeping kitchen	M Ⓢ E	_X_ Yes ____ No	
16)	Taking out garbage	M S Ⓔ	_X_ Yes ____ No	
17)	Washing dishes	M Ⓢ E	_X_ Yes ____ No	
18)	Yard work	M S Ⓔ	_X_ Yes ____ No	
19)	Other _____	M S E	____ Yes ____ No	
20)	Other _____	M S E	____ Yes ____ No	

20) If some of the following behaviors take place only during MILD arguments circle an "M" in the appropriate blanks. If they take place only during SEVERE arguments, circle an "S." If they take place during ALL arguments circle an "A." Fill this out for you and your impression of your spouse. If certain behaviors do not take place, leave them blank.

CIRCLE THE APPROPRIATE RESPONSE FOR EACH.

M=Mild arguments only, **S**=Severe arguments only, **A**=All arguments

BEHAVIOR	BY ME	BY SPOUSE	SHOULD THIS CHANGE?
1) Apologize	M (S) A	M S (A)	_____ Yes _X_ No
2) Become silent	M S A	M S (A)	_X_ Yes _____ No
3) Bring up the past	M S (A)	M (S) A	_X_ Yes _____ No
4) Criticize	M S (A)	M S A	_X_ Yes _____ No
5) Cruel accusations	M (S) A	M S A	_X_ Yes _____ No
6) Cry	M S A	M (S) A	_____ Yes _X_ No
7) Destroy property	M S A	M S A	_____ Yes _____ No
8) Leave the house	M (S) A	M S A	_____ Yes _X_ No
9) Make peace	M S A	M S (A)	_____ Yes _X_ No
10) Moodiness	M S A	M (S) A	_X_ Yes _____ No
11) Not listen	M S (A)	M S (A)	_X_ Yes _____ No
12) Physical abuse	M S A	M S A	_____ Yes _____ No
13) Physical threats	M S A	M S A	_____ Yes _____ No
14) Sarcasm	M S (A)	M S A	_X_ Yes _____ No
15) Scream	M S A	M S A	_____ Yes _____ No
16) Slam doors	M S A	M (S) A	_____ Yes _X_ No
17) Speak irrationally	M S A	M S (A)	_X_ Yes _____ No
18) Speak rationally	M S A	M S (A)	_____ Yes _X_ No
19) Sulk	M S A	M S A	_____ Yes _____ No
20) Swear	M S (A)	M S A	_____ Yes _X_ No
21) Threaten divorce	M (S) A	M S A	_X_ Yes _____ No
22) Threaten to take kids	M S A	M S A	_____ Yes _____ No
23) Throw things	M S A	M S A	_____ Yes _____ No
24) Verbal abuse	M (S) A	M S A	_X_ Yes _____ No
25) Yell	M (S) A	M S A	_X_ Yes _____ No
26) _____	M S A	M S A	_____ Yes _____ No
27) _____	M S A	M S A	_____ Yes _____ No
28) _____	M S A	M S A	_____ Yes _____ No

21) How often do you have

MILD ARGUMENTS? ___4–5 times per week___

SEVERE ARGUMENTS? ___once per week___

22) When a **MILD** argument is over how do you usually feel?

CHECK APPROPRIATE RESPONSES

_X_ Angry	___ Lonely
___ Anxious	___ Nauseous
___ Childish	___ Numb
___ Defeated	___ Regretful
___ Depressed	___ Relieved
___ Guilty	___ Stupid
___ Happy	___ Victimized
___ Hopeless	___ Worthless
_X_ Irritable	

23) When a **SEVERE** argument is over how do you usually feel?

CHECK APPROPRIATE RESPONSES

_X_ Angry	_X_ Lonely
___ Anxious	___ Nauseous
_X_ Childish	_X_ Numb
_X_ Defeated	_X_ Regretful
_X_ Depressed	___ Relieved
_X_ Guilty	_X_ Stupid
___ Happy	_X_ Victimized
___ Hopeless	_X_ Worthless
_X_ Irritable	

24) Which of the following issues or behaviors of you and/or your spouse may be attributable to your marital or personal conflicts? If an item does not apply, leave it blank.
CIRCLE THE APPROPRIATE RESPONSES.

M = My behavior,   **S** = Spouse's behavior,   **B** = Both

Alcohol consumption	M	S	(B)	Perfectionist	M	(S)	B
Childishness	M	S	B	Possessive	M	(S)	B
Controlling	M	S	(B)	Spends too much	(M)	S	B
Defensiveness	M	S	(B)	Steals	M	S	B
Degrading	(M)	S	B	Stubbornness	M	S	(B)
Demanding	M	(S)	B	Uncaring	M	S	B
Drugs	M	S	B	Unstable	M	S	B
Flirts with others	M	(S)	B	Violent	M	S	B
Gambling	M	S	B	Withdrawn	M	S	B
Irresponsibility	M	S	B	Works too much	M	S	(B)
Lies	M	S	B	Other (specify)			
Past marriage(s)	M	(S)	B	_____	M	S	B
Other's advice	M	S	B	_____	M	S	B
Outside interests	M	S	(B)	_____	M	S	B
Past failures	M	S	(B)	_____	M	S	B

25) In the remaining space please provide additional information that would be helpful:

Everyone knows we come from different backgrounds. I believe in living for the moment to enjoy life at its fullest; she believes that everyone has a job and everything has its proper place. If I want to take a trip, I go, but she thinks about it for several months and eventually loses interest, wondering why she never has any fun in life. She believes that I am impulsive, and I believe that she is over-controlled. I give the children freedom, while she says, "Spare the rod and spoil the child." We want to stay together, but we are on different planes. I am a third-generation Korean in the USA, and she is first-generation. This is not Korea, it is the USA.

I, _____*Bobby Chen*_____, hereby give my permission for this clinic to share the information that I provide on this form to _____*Lo Chen*_____ (spouse) when it is deemed appropriate by an agreement between me, my spouse, and our therapist. This sharing of information may take place only during a joint counseling session (both spouses present).

_____*Bobby Chen*_____
Client's Signature

PLEASE RETURN THIS AND OTHER ASSESSMENT MATERIALS TO THIS OFFICE AT LEAST TWO DAYS BEFORE YOUR NEXT APPOINTMENT.

Marital Information Form

1) Name: _____ 2) Age: _____ 3) Date: _____

4) Address: _____
   Street & Number   City   State   Zip

5) Briefly, what is your main purpose in coming to marital therapy?: _____
_____

INSTRUCTIONS: To assist us in helping you, please fill out this form as fully and openly as possible. Your answers will help plan a course of marital therapy that is most suitable for you and your spouse. Do not exchange this information with your spouse.

Several of your answers on this form may be shared later with your spouse during joint therapy sessions if you give us permission to share this information. For this reason you are advised to respond honestly and carefully to each item. If certain questions do not apply to you or you do not want to share this information, please leave them blank.

6) Is this your first marriage?: Yes _____ No _____
   If No, which marriage is it for you?:   2   3   4   5+

7) How long have you and your present spouse been married?: _____

8) Are you and your spouse presently living together?: Yes _____ No _____
   If No, why not?: _____

9) How many times have you and your spouse separated?: _____

10) Fill out the following information for each child of whom the natural parent is both you and your partner, children from previous relationships, and adopted children.

*"Whose Child?" answering options: B=Both of ours, natural child
                                     BA=Both of ours, adopted (or taken on)
                                     M=My natural child
                                     MA=My child, adopted (or taken on)
                                     S=Spouse's natural child
                                     SA=Spouse's child, adopted (or taken on)

Child's Name	Age	Sex	*Whose Child?	Lives with You and Spouse?
1) _____	____	F M	_____	___Yes ___No
2) _____	____	F M	_____	___Yes ___No
3) _____	____	F M	_____	___Yes ___No
4) _____	____	F M	_____	___Yes ___No
5) _____	____	F M	_____	___Yes ___No
6) _____	____	F M	_____	___Yes ___No
7) _____	____	F M	_____	___Yes ___No
8) _____	____	F M	_____	___Yes ___No

11) List five qualities that initially
    attracted you to your spouse:

Does your spouse still
possess this trait?

1) _____ _____ Yes _____No
2) _____ _____ Yes _____No
3) _____ _____ Yes _____No
4) _____ _____ Yes _____No
5) _____ _____ Yes _____No

12) List four negative concerns that
    you initially had in the relationship:

Does your spouse still
possess this trait?

1) _____ _____ Yes _____No
2) _____ _____ Yes _____No
3) _____ _____ Yes _____No
4) _____ _____ Yes _____No

13) List five present positive
    attributes of your spouse:

Do you often praise your
spouse for this trait?

1) _____ _____ Yes _____No
2) _____ _____ Yes _____No
3) _____ _____ Yes _____No
4) _____ _____ Yes _____No
5) _____ _____ Yes _____No

14) List five present negative
    attributes of your spouse:

Do you nag your spouse
about this trait?

1) _____ _____ Yes _____No
2) _____ _____ Yes _____No
3) _____ _____ Yes _____No
4) _____ _____ Yes _____No
5) _____ _____ Yes _____No

15) List five things that you do (or
    could do) to make the marriage
    more fulfilling for your spouse:

Do you often implement
this behavior?

1) _____ _____ Yes _____No
2) _____ _____ Yes _____No
3) _____ _____ Yes _____No
4) _____ _____ Yes _____No
5) _____ _____ Yes _____No

16) List five things that your spouse
    does (or could do) to make the
    marriage more fulfilling for you:

Does your spouse
often implement
this behavior?

1) _____ _____ Yes _____No
2) _____ _____ Yes _____No
3) _____ _____ Yes _____No
4) _____ _____ Yes _____No
5) _____ _____ Yes _____No

17) List five expectations or dreams you had about marriage
    before you married your spouse:

Has this been
fulfilled?

1) _____ _____ Yes _____No
2) _____ _____ Yes _____No
3) _____ _____ Yes _____No
4) _____ _____ Yes _____No
5) _____ _____ Yes _____No

18) On a scale of 1 to 5 rate the following items as they pertain to:

       1) The present state of the marriage
       2) Your need or desire for it
       3) Your spouse's need or desire for it

CIRCLE THE APPROPRIATE RESPONSE FOR EACH

		Present State of the Marriage	Your Need or Desire	Spouse's Need or Desire
		Poor ...... Great	Low ...... High	Low ...... High
1)	Affection	1 2 3 4 5	1 2 3 4 5	1 2 3 4 5
2)	Childrearing rules	1 2 3 4 5	1 2 3 4 5	1 2 3 4 5
3)	Commitment together	1 2 3 4 5	1 2 3 4 5	1 2 3 4 5
4)	Communication	1 2 3 4 5	1 2 3 4 5	1 2 3 4 5
5)	Emotional closeness	1 2 3 4 5	1 2 3 4 5	1 2 3 4 5
6)	Financial security	1 2 3 4 5	1 2 3 4 5	1 2 3 4 5
7)	Honesty	1 2 3 4 5	1 2 3 4 5	1 2 3 4 5
8)	Housework sharing	1 2 3 4 5	1 2 3 4 5	1 2 3 4 5
9)	Love	1 2 3 4 5	1 2 3 4 5	1 2 3 4 5
10)	Physical attraction	1 2 3 4 5	1 2 3 4 5	1 2 3 4 5
11)	Religious commitment	1 2 3 4 5	1 2 3 4 5	1 2 3 4 5
12)	Respect	1 2 3 4 5	1 2 3 4 5	1 2 3 4 5
13)	Sexual fulfillment	1 2 3 4 5	1 2 3 4 5	1 2 3 4 5
14)	Social life together	1 2 3 4 5	1 2 3 4 5	1 2 3 4 5
15)	Time together	1 2 3 4 5	1 2 3 4 5	1 2 3 4 5
16)	Trust	1 2 3 4 5	1 2 3 4 5	1 2 3 4 5
	Other (specify)			
17)	_____	1 2 3 4 5	1 2 3 4 5	1 2 3 4 5
18)	_____	1 2 3 4 5	1 2 3 4 5	1 2 3 4 5
19)	_____	1 2 3 4 5	1 2 3 4 5	1 2 3 4 5
20)	_____	1 2 3 4 5	1 2 3 4 5	1 2 3 4 5

19) Which partner spends more time conducting the following activities?:

CIRCLE THE APPROPRIATE RESPONSE FOR EACH.

M=Me, **S**=Spouse, **E**=Equal time   Is this equitable (fair)?   Comments

		M S E	Is this equitable (fair)?	
1)	Auto repairs	M S E	_____Yes _____No	
2)	Child care	M S E	_____Yes _____No	
3)	Child discipline	M S E	_____Yes _____No	
4)	Cleaning bathrooms	M S E	_____Yes _____No	
5)	Cooking	M S E	_____Yes _____No	
6)	Employment	M S E	_____Yes _____No	
7)	Grocery shopping	M S E	_____Yes _____No	
8)	House cleaning	M S E	_____Yes _____No	
9)	Inside repairs	M S E	_____Yes _____No	
10)	Laundry	M S E	_____Yes _____No	
11)	Making bed	M S E	_____Yes _____No	
12)	Outside repairs	M S E	_____Yes _____No	
13)	Recreational events	M S E	_____Yes _____No	
14)	Social activities	M S E	_____Yes _____No	
15)	Sweeping kitchen	M S E	_____Yes _____No	
16)	Taking out garbage	M S E	_____Yes _____No	
17)	Washing dishes	M S E	_____Yes _____No	
18)	Yard work	M S E	_____Yes _____No	
19)	Other _____	M S E	_____Yes _____No	
20)	Other _____	M S E	_____Yes _____No	

6.11

20) If some of the following behaviors take place only during MILD arguments circle an "M" in the appropriate blanks. If they take place only during SEVERE arguments, circle an "S." If they take place during ALL arguments circle an "A." Fill this out for you and your impression of your spouse. If certain behaviors do not take place, leave them blank.

CIRCLE THE APPROPRIATE RESPONSE FOR EACH.

M=Mild arguments only, **S**=Severe arguments only, **A**=All arguments

BEHAVIOR	BY ME	BY SPOUSE	SHOULD THIS CHANGE?	
1) Apologize	M S A	M S A	____Yes	____No
2) Become silent	M S A	M S A	____Yes	____No
3) Bring up the past	M S A	M S A	____Yes	____No
4) Criticize	M S A	M S A	____Yes	____No
5) Cruel accusations	M S A	M S A	____Yes	____No
6) Cry	M S A	M S A	____Yes	____No
7) Destroy property	M S A	M S A	____Yes	____No
8) Leave the house	M S A	M S A	____Yes	____No
9) Make peace	M S A	M S A	____Yes	____No
10) Moodiness	M S A	M S A	____Yes	____No
11) Not listen	M S A	M S A	____Yes	____No
12) Physical abuse	M S A	M S A	____Yes	____No
13) Physical threats	M S A	M S A	____Yes	____No
14) Sarcasm	M S A	M S A	____Yes	____No
15) Scream	M S A	M S A	____Yes	____No
16) Slam doors	M S A	M S A	____Yes	____No
17) Speak irrationally	M S A	M S A	____Yes	____No
18) Speak rationally	M S A	M S A	____Yes	____No
19) Sulk	M S A	M S A	____Yes	____No
20) Swear	M S A	M S A	____Yes	____No
21) Threaten divorce	M S A	M S A	____Yes	____No
22) Threaten to take kids	M S A	M S A	____Yes	____No
23) Throw things	M S A	M S A	____Yes	____No
24) Verbal abuse	M S A	M S A	____Yes	____No
25) Yell	M S A	M S A	____Yes	____No
26) _____	M S A	M S A	____Yes	____No
27) _____	M S A	M S A	____Yes	____No
28) _____	M S A	M S A	____Yes	____No

21) How often do you have   MILD ARGUMENTS? _____

SEVERE ARGUMENTS? _____

22) When a **MILD** argument is over how do you usually feel?

23) When a **SEVERE** argument is over how do you usually feel?

CHECK APPROPRIATE RESPONSES

___ Angry	___ Lonely	___ Angry	___ Lonely
___ Anxious	___ Nauseous	___ Anxious	___ Nauseous
___ Childish	___ Numb	___ Childish	___ Numb
___ Defeated	___ Regretful	___ Defeated	___ Regretful
___ Depressed	___ Relieved	___ Depressed	___ Relieved
___ Guilty	___ Stupid	___ Guilty	___ Stupid
___ Happy	___ Victimized	___ Happy	___ Victimized
___ Hopeless	___ Worthless	___ Hopeless	___ Worthless
___ Irritable		___ Irritable	

24) Which of the following issues or behaviors of you and/or your spouse may be attributable to your marital or personal conflicts? If an item does not apply, leave it blank.

CIRCLE THE APPROPRIATE RESPONSES.

M = My behavior,   **S** = Spouse's behavior,   **B** = Both

Alcohol consumption	M S B		Perfectionist	M S B
Childishness	M S B		Possessive	M S B
Controlling	M S B		Spends too much	M S B
Defensiveness	M S B		Steals	M S B
Degrading	M S B		Stubbornness	M S B
Demanding	M S B		Uncaring	M S B
Drugs	M S B		Unstable	M S B
Flirts with others	M S B		Violent	M S B
Gambling	M S B		Withdrawn	M S B
Irresponsibility	M S B		Works too much	M S B
Lies	M S B		Other (specify)	
Past marriage(s)	M S B		_____	M S B
Other's advice	M S B		_____	M S B
Outside interests	M S B		_____	M S B
Past failures	M S B		_____	M S B

25) In the remaining space please provide additional information that would be helpful:

_____

_____

_____

_____

_____

_____

_____

_____

_____

_____

_____

_____

_____

_____

I, _____, hereby give my permission for this clinic to share the information that I provide on this form to _____ (spouse) when it is deemed appropriate by an agreement between me, my spouse, and our therapist. This sharing of information may take place only during a joint counseling session (both spouses present).

_____

Client's Signature

PLEASE RETURN THIS AND OTHER ASSESSMENT MATERIALS TO THIS
OFFICE AT LEAST TWO DAYS BEFORE YOUR NEXT APPOINTMENT.

Couple's Information Form

1) Name: _Danielle Barnes_   2) Age: _28_   3) Date: _5-6-97_

4) Address: _76543 2nd St._   _Boomington_   _MN_   _98765_
   Street & Number   City   State   Zip

5) Briefly, what is your main purpose in coming to couple's counseling? _Considering_ _marriage, but my fiance has problems with alcohol. I'm not sure whether I can handle this_ _for the rest of my life._

INSTRUCTIONS: To assist us in helping you, please fill out this form as fully and openly as possible. Your answers will help plan a course of couple's therapy that is most suitable for you and your partner. Do not exchange this information with your partner at this time.

Several of your answers on this form may be shared later with your partner during joint therapy sessions if you give us permission to share this information. For this reason you are advised to respond honestly and carefully to each item. If certain questions do not apply to you or you do not want to share this information, please leave them blank.

6) Have you been married before?:   Yes _X_   No _____

   If Yes, how many previous marriages have you had?:   ①   2   3   4   5+

7) How long have you and your partner been in this relationship?:   _2 years_

8) Are you and your partner presently living together?:   Yes _X_   No _____

9) Are you and your partner engaged to be married?: Yes, _X_ When? _3 months_ No _____

10) Fill out the following information for each child of whom the natural parent is both you and your partner, children from previous relationships, and adopted children.

    _____ Neither of us has children (go to next page)   _X_ One or each of us has children (continue)

*"Whose Child?" answering options: B=Both of ours, natural child
                                        BA=Both of ours, adopted (or taken on)
                                        M=My natural child
                                        MA=My child, adopted (or taken on)
                                        P=Partner's natural child
                                        PA=Partner's child, adopted (or taken on)

Child's Name	Age	Sex	*Whose Child?	Lives with Whom?
1) _Lisa_	_4_	Ⓕ M	_M_	_Me_
2) _____	___	F M	_____	_____
3) _____	___	F M	_____	_____
4) _____	___	F M	_____	_____
5) _____	___	F M	_____	_____
6) _____	___	F M	_____	_____
7) _____	___	F M	_____	_____
8) _____	___	F M	_____	_____

11) List five qualities that initially
attracted you to your partner:

      1) _Good listener_

      2) _He flirted with me_

      3) _Good looking_

      4) _He has several friends_

      5) _He understands me_

Does your partner still possess this trait?

  __X__ Yes _____ No
  __X__ Yes _____ No
  __X__ Yes _____ No
  __X__ Yes _____ No
  __X__ Yes _____ No

12) List four negative concerns that
you initially had in the relationship:

      1) _Spending money unwisely_

      2) _Alcohol consumption_

      3) _Lying to his boss at work when hung over_

      4) _Coming home late in the evening with excuses_

Does your partner still possess this trait?

  __X__ Yes _____ No
  __X__ Yes _____ No
  __X__ Yes _____ No
  __X__ Yes _____ No

13) List five present positive
attributes of your partner:

      1) _Good provider_

      2) _Works hard_

      3) _Good to my child_

      4) _Wants me to be happy_

      5) _Friendly to my family_

Do you often praise your partner for this trait?

  __X__ Yes _____ No
  _____ Yes __X__ No
  __X__ Yes _____ No
  _____ Yes __X__ No
  __X__ Yes _____ No

14) List five present negative
attributes of your partner:

      1) _Drinks too much alcohol_

      2) _Will not go to AA or counseling_

      3) _Denies his alcohol problem_

      4) _Spends too much money, doesn't save_

      5) _Tries too hard to please most people_

Do you nag your partner about this trait?

  __X__ Yes _____ No
  __X__ Yes _____ No
  __X__ Yes _____ No
  __X__ Yes _____ No
  _____ Yes __X__ No

15) List five things that you do (or
could do) to make your relationship
more fulfilling for your partner:

      1) _Let him know that I care about his health_

      2) _Listen to his opinions_

      3) _Tell him I love him_

      4) _Acknowledge that he is quite stressed_

      5) _____

Do you often implement this behavior?

  _____ Yes __X__ No
  __X__ Yes _____ No
  __X__ Yes _____ No
  _____ Yes __X__ No
  _____ Yes _____ No

16) List five things that your partner
does (or could do) to make the
relationship more fulfilling for you:

      1) _Stop drinking alcohol_

      2) _Respect my opinions_

      3) _Treat my child and family well_

      4) _Go to religious services with me_

      5) _____

Does your partner often implement this behavior?

  _____ Yes __X__ No
  __X__ Yes _____ No
  __X__ Yes _____ No
  $\frac{1}{2}$ Yes $\frac{1}{2}$ No
  _____ Yes _____ No

17) List five expectations or dreams you had about relationships
before you met your partner:

      1) _Respect each other_

      2) _Functional family_

      3) _No chemical dependency issues_

      4) _Feel loved_

      5) _Financial freedom_

Has this been fulfilled?

  _____ Yes __X__ No
  _____ Yes __X__ No
  _____ Yes __X__ No
  __X__ Yes _____ No
  __X__ Yes _____ No

18) On a scale of 1 to 5 rate the following items as they pertain to:
         1)   The present state of the relationship
         2)   Your need or desire for it
         3)   Your partner's need or desire for it

CIRCLE THE APPROPRIATE RESPONSE FOR EACH. (If not applicable, leave blank.)

	Present State of the Relationship (Poor–Great)	Your Need or Desire (Low–High)	Partner's Need or Desire (Low–High)
1) Affection	1 2 3 (4) 5	1 2 3 (4) 5	1 2 3 (4) 5
2) Childrearing rules	1 2 3 (4) 5	1 2 3 (4) 5	1 2 3 (4) 5
3) Commitment together	1 2 3 (4) 5	1 2 3 (4) 5	1 2 (3) 4 5
4) Communication	1 2 3 (4) 5	1 2 3 (4) 5	1 2 3 4 5
5) Emotional closeness	1 2 3 (4) 5	1 2 3 (4) 5	1 2 (3) 4 5
6) Financial security	1 2 3 4 (5)	1 2 3 4 (5)	1 (2) 3 4 5
7) Honesty	1 2 3 (4) 5	1 2 3 (4) 5	1 2 (3) 4 5
8) Housework shared	1 2 3 (4) 5	1 2 3 (4) 5	1 2 (3) 4 5
9) Love	1 2 3 (4) 5	1 2 3 (4) 5	1 2 3 (4) 5
10) Physical attraction	1 2 3 (4) 5	1 2 (3) 4 5	1 2 3 (4) 5
11) Religious commitment	1 2 (3) 4 5	1 2 (3) 4 5	1 2 (3) 4 5
12) Respect	1 2 (3) 4 5	1 2 3 (4) 5	1 2 (3) 4 5
13) Sexual fulfillment	1 2 (3) 4 5	1 2 3 4 5	1 2 3 4 5
14) Social life together	1 2 3 (4) 5	1 (2) 3 4 5	1 2 3 4 (5)
15) Time together	1 (2) 3 4 5	1 2 3 (4) 5	1 (2) 3 4 5
16) Trust	1 2 (3) 4 5	1 2 3 4 (5)	1 2 (3) 4 5
Other (specify)			
17) _____	1 2 3 4 5	1 2 3 4 5	1 2 3 4 5
18) _____	1 2 3 4 5	1 2 3 4 5	1 2 3 4 5
19) _____	1 2 3 4 5	1 2 3 4 5	1 2 3 4 5
20) _____	1 2 3 4 5	1 2 3 4 5	1 2 3 4 5

19) FOR COUPLES LIVING TOGETHER. Which partner spends the most time conducting the following activities?:

CIRCLE THE APPROPRIATE RESPONSE FOR EACH. (If not applicable, leave blank.)

M = Me,   **P** = Partner,   **E** = Equal time   Is this equitable (fair)?

	Activity	M P E	Yes	No
1)	Auto repairs	M (P) E	X Yes	___ No
2)	Child care	M P (E)	X Yes	___ No
3)	Child discipline	M P (E)	X Yes	___ No
4)	Cleaning bathrooms	M P (E)	X Yes	___ No
5)	Cooking	M P (E)	X Yes	___ No
6)	Employment	M P (E)	X Yes	___ No
7)	Grocery shopping	(M) P E	X Yes	___ No
8)	House cleaning	M P (E)	X Yes	___ No
9)	Inside repairs	M (P) E	X Yes	___ No
10)	Laundry	(M) P E	X Yes	___ No
11)	Making bed	M P (E)	X Yes	___ No
12)	Outside repairs	M (P) E	X Yes	___ No
13)	Recreational events	M P (E)	X Yes	___ No
14)	Social activities	M (P) E	___ Yes	X No
15)	Sweeping kitchen	(M) P E	X Yes	___ No
16)	Taking out garbage	M P (E)	X Yes	___ No
17)	Washing dishes	M P (E)	X Yes	___ No
18)	Yard work	M (P) E	X Yes	___ No
19)	Other _____	M S E	___ Yes	___ No
20)	Other _____	M S E	___ Yes	___ No

20) If some of the following behaviors take place only during MILD arguments circle an "M" in the appropriate blanks. If they take place only during SEVERE arguments, circle an "S." If they take place during ALL arguments circle an "A." Fill this out for you and your impression of your spouse. If certain behaviors do not take place, leave them blank.

CIRCLE THE APPROPRIATE RESPONSE FOR EACH.

M=Mild arguments only, **S**=Severe arguments only, **A**=All arguments

BEHAVIOR	BY ME	BY SPOUSE	SHOULD THIS CHANGE?	
1) Apologize	M S Ⓐ	M S A	X Yes	No
2) Become silent	M S A	M S Ⓐ	X Yes	No
3) Bring up the past	M Ⓢ A	M S A	X Yes	No
4) Criticize	M Ⓢ A	M Ⓢ A	X Yes	No
5) Cruel accusations	M Ⓢ A	M S A	X Yes	No
6) Cry	M S A	M S A	Yes	X No
7) Destroy property	M S A	M S A	Yes	X No
8) Leave the house	M Ⓢ Ⓐ	M S Ⓐ	X Yes	No
9) Make peace	M S Ⓐ	M S A	X Yes	No
10) Moodiness	M Ⓢ A	M Ⓢ A	X Yes	No
11) Not listen	M S A	M S A	Yes	X No
12) Physical abuse	M S A	M S A	Yes	X No
13) Physical threats	M S A	M S A	Yes	X No
14) Sarcasm	M Ⓢ A	M S A	X Yes	No
15) Scream	M S A	M S A	Yes	X No
16) Slam doors	M S A	M S A	Yes	X No
17) Speak irrationally	M S A	M S A	Yes	X No
18) Speak rationally	M S Ⓐ	M S Ⓐ	Yes	X No
19) Sulk	M S A	M S A	Yes	X No
20) Swear	M Ⓢ A	M S A	Yes	X No
21) Threaten divorce	M S Ⓐ	M S A	X Yes	No
22) Threaten to take kids	M S A	M S A	Yes	X No
23) Throw things	M S A	M S A	Yes	X No
24) Verbal abuse	M S A	M S A	Yes	X No
25) Yell	M S A	M S A	Yes	X No
26) _____	M S A	M S A	Yes	No
27) _____	M S A	M S A	Yes	No
28) _____	M S A	M S A	Yes	No

21) How often do you have MILD ARGUMENTS? _Once/week_

SEVERE ARGUMENTS? _2–3/year_

22) When a **MILD** argument is over how do you usually feel?

CHECK APPROPRIATE RESPONSES

X Angry	___ Lonely
X Anxious	___ Nauseous
___ Childish	___ Numb
___ Defeated	___ Regretful
___ Depressed	X Relieved
___ Guilty	___ Stupid
___ Happy	___ Victimized
___ Hopeless	___ Worthless
X Irritable	

23) When a **SEVERE** argument is over how do you usually feel?

CHECK APPROPRIATE RESPONSES

X Angry	___ Lonely
X Anxious	___ Nauseous
___ Childish	X Numb
X Defeated	X Regretful
___ Depressed	___ Relieved
X Guilty	___ Stupid
___ Happy	___ Victimized
___ Hopeless	X Worthless
X Irritable	

24) Which of the following issues or behaviors of you and/or your partner may be attributable to your marital or personal conflicts? If an item does not apply, leave it blank.
CIRCLE THE APPROPRIATE RESPONSES.

M = My behavior, **S** = Partner's behavior, **B** = Both

Alcohol consumption	M (P) B	Perfectionist	M P (B)
Childishness	M P B	Possessive	(M) P B
Controlling	(M) P B	Spends too much money	M (P) B
Defensiveness	M (P) B	Steals	M P B
Degrading	M P B	Stubbornness	M P B
Demanding	(M) P B	Uncaring	M P B
Drugs	M P B	Unstable	M P B
Flirts with others	M P B	Violent	M P B
Gambling	M P B	Withdrawn	M P B
Irresponsibility	M (P) B	Works too much	M P (B)
Lies	M (P) B	Other (specify)	
Past marriage(s)/relationship(s)	M P B	_____	M P B
Other's advice	M (P) B	_____	M P B
Outside interests	M (P) B	_____	M P B
Past failures	M P B	_____	M P B

25) In the remaining space please provide additional information that would be helpful:

Most people think that we have the perfect relationship. My friends jokingly say, "If you ever break up, he's mine." He is a very caring man, but his drinking is too much. When I grew up I saw the same thing happen to my parents, plus, in my first marriage, alcoholism ruined everything. He believes that I am paranoid about anyone who drinks alcohol and the problem is really mine. He even told me it might be helpful for me to attend counseling to deal with my past (abuse by alcoholic father and ex-spouse). His amount of drinking seems to increase steadily. Although he usually doesn't miss work, I've noticed that he cares less about his career than when we first met. He seems to look forward to going to the bar after work with his friends to "discuss work." He is not a bad person, but what if things get worse? Will my child and I suffer again through another mess?

I, ___*Danielle Barnes*___ , hereby give my permission for ___*The Counseling Clinic*___ to share the information that I provide on this form to ___*Herbert Heathcolte*___ (partner) when it is deemed appropriate by an agreement between me, my partner, and our therapist. This sharing of information may take place only during a joint counseling session (both partners present).

___*Danielle Barnes*___
Client's Signature

**PLEASE RETURN THIS AND OTHER ASSESSMENT MATERIALS TO THIS
OFFICE AT LEAST TWO DAYS BEFORE YOUR NEXT APPOINTMENT.**

Couple's Information Form

1) Name: _____ 2) Age:_____ 3) Date: _____
4) Address: _____
              Street & Number   City   State   Zip
5) Briefly, what is your main purpose in coming to couple's counseling? _____
    _____
    _____

INSTRUCTIONS: To assist us in helping you, please fill out this form as fully and openly as possible. Your answers will help plan a course of couple's therapy that is most suitable for you and your partner. Do not exchange this information with your partner at this time.

Several of your answers on this form may be shared later with your partner during joint therapy sessions if you give us permission to share this information. For this reason you are advised to respond honestly and carefully to each item. If certain questions do not apply to you or you do not want to share this information, please leave them blank.

6) Have you been married before?:   Yes _____   No _____
    If Yes, how many previous marriages have you had?:   1   2   3   4   5+
7) How long have you and your partner been in this relationship?:   _____
8) Are you and your partner presently living together?:   Yes _____   No _____
9) Are you and your partner engaged to be married?: Yes, _____ When? _____ No _____
10) Fill out the following information for each child of whom the natural parent is both you and
    your partner, children from previous relationships, and adopted children.
    _____ Neither of us has children (go to next page)   _____ One or each of us has children (continue)

*"Whose Child?" answering options: B=Both of ours, natural child
                                       BA=Both of ours, adopted (or taken on)
                                       M=My natural child
                                       MA=My child, adopted (or taken on)
                                       P=Partner's natural child
                                       PA=Partner's child, adopted (or taken on)

Child's Name	Age	Sex	*Whose Child?	Lives with Whom?
1) _____	_____	F M	_____	_____
2) _____	_____	F M	_____	_____
3) _____	_____	F M	_____	_____
4) _____	_____	F M	_____	_____
5) _____	_____	F M	_____	_____
6) _____	_____	F M	_____	_____
7) _____	_____	F M	_____	_____
8) _____	_____	F M	_____	_____

11) List five qualities that initially
attracted you to your partner:

Does your partner still
possess this trait?

1) _____   _____Yes _____No
2) _____   _____Yes _____No
3) _____   _____Yes _____No
4) _____   _____Yes _____No
5) _____   _____Yes _____No

12) List four negative concerns that
you initially had in the relationship:

Does your partner still
possess this trait?

1) _____   _____Yes _____No
2) _____   _____Yes _____No
3) _____   _____Yes _____No
4) _____   _____Yes _____No

13) List five present positive
attributes of your partner:

Do you often praise your
partner for this trait?

1) _____   _____Yes _____No
2) _____   _____Yes _____No
3) _____   _____Yes _____No
4) _____   _____Yes _____No
5) _____   _____Yes _____No

14) List five present negative
attributes of your partner:

Do you nag your partner
about this trait?

1) _____   _____Yes _____No
2) _____   _____Yes _____No
3) _____   _____Yes _____No
4) _____   _____Yes _____No
5) _____   _____Yes _____No

15) List five things that you do (or
could do) to make your relationship
more fulfilling for your partner:

Do you often implement
this behavior?

1) _____   _____Yes _____No
2) _____   _____Yes _____No
3) _____   _____Yes _____No
4) _____   _____Yes _____No
5) _____   _____Yes _____No

16) List five things that your partner
does (or could do) to make the
relationship more fulfilling for you:

Does your partner
often implement
this behavior?

1) _____   _____Yes _____No
2) _____   _____Yes _____No
3) _____   _____Yes _____No
4) _____   _____Yes _____No
5) _____   _____Yes _____No

17) List five expectations or dreams you had about relationships
before you met your partner:

Has this been
fulfilled?

1) _____   _____Yes _____No
2) _____   _____Yes _____No
3) _____   _____Yes _____No
4) _____   _____Yes _____No
5) _____   _____Yes _____No

18) On a scale of 1 to 5 rate the following items as they pertain to:
                1)   The present state of the relationship
                2)   Your need or desire for it
                3)   Your partner's need or desire for it

CIRCLE THE APPROPRIATE RESPONSE FOR EACH. (If not applicable, leave blank.)

	Present State of the Relationship	Your Need or Desire	Partner's Need or Desire
	Poor Great	Low High	Low High
1) Affection	1 2 3 4 5	1 2 3 4 5	1 2 3 4 5
2) Childrearing rules	1 2 3 4 5	1 2 3 4 5	1 2 3 4 5
3) Commitment together	1 2 3 4 5	1 2 3 4 5	1 2 3 4 5
4) Communication	1 2 3 4 5	1 2 3 4 5	1 2 3 4 5
5) Emotional closeness	1 2 3 4 5	1 2 3 4 5	1 2 3 4 5
6) Financial security	1 2 3 4 5	1 2 3 4 5	1 2 3 4 5
7) Honesty	1 2 3 4 5	1 2 3 4 5	1 2 3 4 5
8) Housework shared	1 2 3 4 5	1 2 3 4 5	1 2 3 4 5
9) Love	1 2 3 4 5	1 2 3 4 5	1 2 3 4 5
10) Physical attraction	1 2 3 4 5	1 2 3 4 5	1 2 3 4 5
11) Religious commitment	1 2 3 4 5	1 2 3 4 5	1 2 3 4 5
12) Respect	1 2 3 4 5	1 2 3 4 5	1 2 3 4 5
13) Sexual fulfillment	1 2 3 4 5	1 2 3 4 5	1 2 3 4 5
14) Social life together	1 2 3 4 5	1 2 3 4 5	1 2 3 4 5
15) Time together	1 2 3 4 5	1 2 3 4 5	1 2 3 4 5
16) Trust	1 2 3 4 5	1 2 3 4 5	1 2 3 4 5
Other (specify)			
17) _____	1 2 3 4 5	1 2 3 4 5	1 2 3 4 5
18) _____	1 2 3 4 5	1 2 3 4 5	1 2 3 4 5
19) _____	1 2 3 4 5	1 2 3 4 5	1 2 3 4 5
20) _____	1 2 3 4 5	1 2 3 4 5	1 2 3 4 5

19) FOR COUPLES LIVING TOGETHER. Which partner spends the most time conducting the following activities?:

CIRCLE THE APPROPRIATE RESPONSE FOR EACH. (If not applicable, leave blank.)
M = Me,   **P** = Partner,   **E** = Equal time   Is this equitable (fair)?

			Yes	No
1) Auto repairs	M P E		_____Yes	_____No
2) Child care	M P E		_____Yes	_____No
3) Child discipline	M P E		_____Yes	_____No
4) Cleaning bathrooms	M P E		_____Yes	_____No
5) Cooking	M P E		_____Yes	_____No
6) Employment	M P E		_____Yes	_____No
7) Grocery shopping	M P E		_____Yes	_____No
8) House cleaning	M P E		_____Yes	_____No
9) Inside repairs	M P E		_____Yes	_____No
10) Laundry	M P E		_____Yes	_____No
11) Making bed	M P E		_____Yes	_____No
12) Outside repairs	M P E		_____Yes	_____No
13) Recreational events	M P E		_____Yes	_____No
14) Social activities	M P E		_____Yes	_____No
15) Sweeping kitchen	M P E		_____Yes	_____No
16) Taking out garbage	M P E		_____Yes	_____No
17) Washing dishes	M P E		_____Yes	_____No
18) Yard work	M P E		_____Yes	_____No
19) Other _____	M S E		_____Yes	_____No
20) Other _____	M S E		_____Yes	_____No

6.21

20) If some of the following behaviors take place only during MILD arguments circle an "M" in the appropriate blanks. If they take place only during SEVERE arguments, circle an "S." If they take place during ALL arguments, circle an "A." Fill this out for you and your impression of your spouse. If certain behaviors do not take place, leave them blank.

CIRCLE THE APPROPRIATE RESPONSE FOR EACH.

M = Mild arguments only,   **S** = Severe arguments only,   **A** = All arguments

BEHAVIOR	BY ME	BY PARTNER	SHOULD THIS CHANGE?	
1) Apologize	M S A	M S A	____Yes	____No
2) Become silent	M S A	M S A	____Yes	____No
3) Bring up the past	M S A	M S A	____Yes	____No
4) Criticize	M S A	M S A	____Yes	____No
5) Cruel accusations	M S A	M S A	____Yes	____No
6) Cry	M S A	M S A	____Yes	____No
7) Destroy property	M S A	M S A	____Yes	____No
8) Leave the house	M S A	M S A	____Yes	____No
9) Make peace	M S A	M S A	____Yes	____No
10) Moodines	M S A	M S A	____Yes	____No
11) Not listen	M S A	M S A	____Yes	____No
12) Physical abuse	M S A	M S A	____Yes	____No
13) Physical threats	M S A	M S A	____Yes	____No
14) Sarcasm	M S A	M S A	____Yes	____No
15) Scream	M S A	M S A	____Yes	____No
16) Slam doors	M S A	M S A	____Yes	____No
17) Speak irrationally	M S A	M S A	____Yes	____No
18) Speak rationally	M S A	M S A	____Yes	____No
19) Sulk	M S A	M S A	____Yes	____No
20) Swear	M S A	M S A	____Yes	____No
21) Threaten breaking up	M S A	M S A	____Yes	____No
22) Threaten to take kids	M S A	M S A	____Yes	____No
23) Throw things	M S A	M S A	____Yes	____No
24) Verbal abuse	M S A	M S A	____Yes	____No
25) Yell	M S A	M S A	____Yes	____No
26) _____	M S A	M S A	____Yes	____No
27) _____	M S A	M S A	____Yes	____No
28) _____	M S A	M S A	____Yes	____No

21) How often do you have   MILD ARGUMENTS? _____
SEVERE ARGUMENTS? _____

22) When a **MILD** argument is over how do you usually feel?

23) When a **SEVERE** argument is over how do you usually feel?

CHECK APPROPRIATE RESPONSES

___ Angry   ___ Lonely
___ Anxious   ___ Nauseous
___ Childish   ___ Numb
___ Defeated   ___ Regretful
___ Depressed   ___ Relieved
___ Guilty   ___ Stupid
___ Happy   ___ Victimized
___ Hopeless   ___ Worthless
___ Irritable

CHECK APPROPRIATE RESPONSES

___ Angry   ___ Lonely
___ Anxious   ___ Nauseous
___ Childish   ___ Numb
___ Defeated   ___ Regretful
___ Depressed   ___ Relieved
___ Guilty   ___ Stupid
___ Happy   ___ Victimized
___ Hopeless   ___ Worthless
___ Irritable

6.22

24) Which of the following issues or behaviors of you and/or your partner may be attributable to your relationship or personal conflicts? If an item does not apply, leave it blank.
CIRCLE THE APPROPRIATE RESPONSES.

M = My behavior,   **S** = Partner's behavior,   **B** = Both

Alcohol consumption	M P B		Perfectionist	M P B
Childishness	M P B		Possessive	M P B
Controlling	M P B		Spends too much money	M P B
Defensiveness	M P B		Steals	M P B
Degrading	M P B		Stubbornness	M P B
Demanding	M P B		Uncaring	M P B
Drugs	M P B		Unstable	M P B
Flirts with others	M P B		Violent	M P B
Gambling	M P B		Withdrawn	M P B
Irresponsibility	M P B		Works too much	M P B
Lies	M P B		Other (specify)	
Past marriage(s)/relationship(s)	M P B		_____	M P B
Other's advice	M P B		_____	M P B
Outside interests	M P B		_____	M P B
Past failures	M P B		_____	M P B

25) In the remaining space please provide additional information that would be helpful:

_____
_____
_____
_____
_____
_____
_____
_____
_____
_____
_____
_____
_____
_____
_____

I, _____, hereby give my permission for _____ to share the information that I provide on this form to _____ (partner) when it is deemed appropriate by an agreement between me, my partner, and our therapist. This sharing of information may take place only during a joint counseling session (both partners present).

_____
Client's Signature

PLEASE RETURN THIS AND OTHER ASSESSMENT MATERIALS TO THIS
OFFICE AT LEAST TWO DAYS BEFORE YOUR NEXT APPOINTMENT.

Analysis of
Target Behaviors

The Analysis of Target Behaviors form on page 6.25 is designed to increase communication by breaking down negative behaviors in the relationship into causal and affective components. In this homework assignment, clients are asked to indicate how they believe their partner felt after each disagreement and also to list positive alternative actions that could have been taken in place of the negative behavior.

Analysis of Target Behaviors

Your Name: _____Linda Schommer_____ Date: ___3-9-97_____

Spouse's Name: _____Paul Schommer_____

Every couple encounters misunderstandings, disagreements, hurt, and anger, as well as happy times, fulfillment, encouragement, and cooperation. Unfortunately, when relationships are on the down side, too many people dwell on the negatives. Not all people intentionally try to hurt their partners, but, when arguments heat up, they often fall back into selfish attitudes and behaviors that only serve as ammunition for their own cause. Such defenses never facilitate a happy relationship.

A few examples of detrimental behaviors include the following:

- BELITTLING/PUTTING DOWN
- BLAMING OR ACCUSING
- BRINGING UP THE PAST
- CONSTANTLY REFUSING SEX
- CONTROLLING
- DWELLING ON NEGATIVES
- FLIRTING WITH OTHERS
- GUILT TRIPS
- LACK OF AFFECTION
- LYING
- NOT SHARING RESPONSIBILITIES

- PHYSICAL ABUSE
- POUTING
- REFUSING TO TALK/SHUNNING
- SARCASM
- SHIFTING ATTENTION TO FAMILY/FRIENDS
- SPENDING OR HOARDING MONEY
- SUBSTANCE ABUSE
- THREATENING SUICIDE
- THREATENING TO LEAVE
- VERBAL ABUSE
- YELLING

Enjoying a successful relationship involves much more than simply eliminating negative behaviors. Some couples would leave therapy with little to talk about if the counseling only involved discarding the negative. Mutually rewarding, positive actions must replace the negative.

DIRECTIONS: During the next week list all interactions between you and your partner in which negative interactions (such as those above) take place. Mark down the day and approximate time when each take place. Do not share this list with your partner or compare notes. We will go over the lists in the next counseling session. Use as many of the attached sheets as necessary.

This list must contain behaviors acted out by you, your partner, and both. The purpose of this exercise is to learn about and enrich your relationship, not to blame or find fault. We are not interested in determining "who is right," but rather "what is right" for your relationship.

Also include alternative positive actions that could have been taken instead of the negative behavior, and what seemed to cause the behavior (if you know).

DATE: _3-12-97_____   TIME: _____6:45 a.m._____

NEGATIVE BEHAVIOR(S): _Paul kept telling me that the only reason I spend so much time_ _getting ready in the morning is to impress the men at work. Even though there are no_ _other men, I told him, "At least some people care about me."_

ACTED OUT BY WHOM? _____   BOTH _X___

WHAT CAUSED IT TO HAPPEN?: _When pressures between us build up we become quite sarcastic_ _and belittling of each other. When he accuses me I don't try to reason, but rather I try to_ _hurt his feelings and make him feel inadequate._

HOW DID YOU FEEL AFTERWARD?: _Guilty for implying I might have admirers and good_ _because I was one up on him._

HOW DO YOU THINK YOUR PARTNER FELT AFTERWARD?: _Angry and put down._

WHAT POSITIVE ACTIONS COULD HAVE BEEN TAKEN INSTEAD OF THE NEGATIVE?: _We could each let the other know on a regular basis how important we are to each other._ _When I feel like I'm being put down, I could discuss my feelings with him rather than_ _spout off. He could avoid making judgmental statements about me by telling me when is is down._

DATE: _____3-15-97_____   TIME: _____8:30 p.m._____
NEGATIVE BEHAVIOR(S): _He yelled at me for spending $200 on a new outfit. I shouted_ _back that he is not my father and I can spend what I want. Then I drove off and did_ _not come back until 3:00 a.m. and said, "I went where people appreciate me."_

ACTED OUT BY WHOM? _____   BOTH _X___

WHAT CAUSED IT TO HAPPEN?: _We have several unpaid bills, but I spent $200 on a whim. He_ _was very upset and I reacted._

HOW DID YOU FEEL AFTERWARD?: _Angry because he has no right to tell me how much I_ _can spend. Guilty, because we are in debt. Childish, because he lectured me._

HOW DO YOU THINK YOUR PARTNER FELT AFTERWARD?: _Frustrated, because I often_ _overspend when we have other bills to pay._

WHAT POSITIVE ACTIONS COULD HAVE BEEN TAKEN INSTEAD OF THE NEGATIVE?: _This could have been prevented if we had an agreed-on budget. He didn't have to yell at me._ _I didn't have to drive off for several hours. We should agree on expenditures over a certain_ _amount._

6.26

Analysis of Target Behaviors

Your Name: _____ Date:

_____

Spouse's Name: _____

Every couple encounters misunderstandings, disagreements, hurt, and anger, as well as happy times, fulfillment, encouragement, and cooperation. Unfortunately, when relationships are on the down side, too many people dwell on the negatives. Not all people intentionally try to hurt their partners, but, when arguments heat up, they often fall back into selfish attitudes and behaviors that only serve as ammunition for their own cause. Such defenses never facilitate a happy relationship.

A few examples of detrimental behaviors include the following:

- BELITTLING/PUTTING DOWN
- BLAMING OR ACCUSING
- BRINGING UP THE PAST
- CONSTANTLY REFUSING SEX
- CONTROLLING
- DWELLING ON NEGATIVES
- FLIRTING WITH OTHERS
- GUILT TRIPS
- LACK OF AFFECTION
- LYING
- NOT SHARING RESPONSIBILITIES

- PHYSICAL ABUSE
- POUTING
- REFUSING TO TALK/SHUNNING
- SARCASM
- SHIFTING ATTENTION TO FAMILY/FRIENDS
- SPENDING OR HOARDING MONEY
- SUBSTANCE ABUSE
- THREATENING SUICIDE
- THREATENING TO LEAVE
- VERBAL ABUSE
- YELLING

Enjoying a successful relationship involves much more than simply eliminating negative behaviors. Some couples would leave therapy with little to talk about if the counseling only involved discarding the negative. Mutually rewarding, positive actions must replace the negative.

DIRECTIONS: During the next week list all interactions between you and your partner in which negative interactions (such as those above) take place. Mark down the day and approximate time when each take place. Do not share this list with your partner or compare notes. We will go over the lists in the next counseling session. Use as many of the attached sheets as necessary.

This list must contain behaviors acted out by you, your partner, and both. The purpose of this exercise is to learn about and enrich your relationship, not to blame or find fault. We are not interested in determining "who is right," but rather "what is right" for your relationship.

Also include alternative positive actions that could have been taken instead of the negative behavior, and

DATE: _____ TIME: _____

NEGATIVE BEHAVIOR(S): _____
_____
_____

ACTED OUT BY WHOM? _____ BOTH _____

WHAT CAUSED IT TO HAPPEN?: _____
_____
_____

HOW DID YOU FEEL AFTERWARD?: _____
_____

HOW DO YOU THINK YOUR PARTNER FELT AFTERWARD?: _____
_____

WHAT POSITIVE ACTIONS COULD HAVE BEEN TAKEN INSTEAD OF THE NEGATIVE?:
_____
_____
_____

DATE: _____ TIME: _____
NEGATIVE BEHAVIOR(S): _____
_____
_____

ACTED OUT BY WHOM? _____ BOTH _____

WHAT CAUSED IT TO HAPPEN?: _____
_____
_____

HOW DID YOU FEEL AFTERWARD?: _____
_____

HOW DO YOU THINK YOUR PARTNER FELT AFTERWARD?: _____
_____

WHAT POSITIVE ACTIONS COULD HAVE BEEN TAKEN INSTEAD OF THE NEGATIVE?:
_____
_____
_____

Cooperating in Child Rearing

This form begins on page 6.30 with a narrative regarding various reasons why parents' diverse backgrounds and personalities may make it difficult for them to agree on child-rearing practices, followed by a discussion regarding various ways in which the parents may have been raised and how the disparity could cause conflict with the partner's view of parenting. In a homework assignment, each partner is asked to provide information regarding his or her upbringing compared to the partner's. Understanding and compromises are subsequently suggested.

Cooperating in Child Rearing

No two people totally agree on all child-rearing principles. The same individual will often seem strict in some matters but quite lax in others. What you view as strict may be thought of as lenient by your partner. What you consider to be fun might be seen as dangerous by your partner.

Most parents tend to raise their children in a similar manner to how they grew up. Of course there are exceptions, but many of the child-rearing techniques we use were learned because our parents (by their example) taught them to us. Unless your parents were just like your partner's parents, your schooling was identical to your partner's schooling, your ideas are the same as your partner's ideas, and so forth, it is inevitable that some of your child-rearing techniques will conflict with those of your partner.

Two important issues involved in child-rearing practices include:

1) the degree of **warmth vs. hostility** in the household, and
2) the degree of **independence vs. control** rendered to the child.

1) WARMTH VS. HOSTILITY. The amount of warmth shown in a family can range from extremely warm (too much smothering and affection) to extremely hostile (little or no love shown).

Extremely warm families often smother their children with so much affection that the children may grow up demanding that others take care of their needs. If you were raised in an extremely warm family it is possible that you might have some difficulties separating your identity from that of your children and family.

Being raised in a warm, loving family can be quite rewarding provided that it doesn't lead to constant smothering. Warm families tend to be affectionate, accepting, and low in physical punishment; parents don't openly criticize one another and are family-centered, rather than self-centered.

Extremely hostile families are often prone to extreme disciplinary measures toward their children. The words "I love you" are rarely spoken. Parents are often rejecting, cold, disapproving, and quite critical of family members. If you were raised in a hostile family it is possible that you might have some difficulties listening to your children's points of view, showing affection, and controlling your temper.

Some families seem to go back and forth between warmth and hostility. When things are going quite well (e.g., children are obeying, finances are in order, parents are getting along, etc.) these families tend to be warm. But when pressures confront the family, there may be times when the parents vent their hostilities on each other and/or the children. This type of situation becomes confusing to the children because of the mixed messages they are receiving. These parents must learn how to be consistent.

2) INDEPENDENCE VS. CONTROL. The amount of independence granted to children can range from extreme independence (children having few or no rules) to extreme control (children allowed to make few or no decisions).

Extreme independence in a family allows the children to do almost whatever they want to do. Parents reason that the children will learn from their mistakes and grow from the experiences. Few restrictions are imposed, and little enforcement is provided for these restrictions. If you were raised in an extremely independent child-rearing family, it is quite possible that you are somewhat uncomfortable when it comes to setting limits or enforcing family rules.

Extreme control in a family allows few decisions to be made without the approval of the "head of the house." Children are expected to do exactly what they are told, even when no logical reason is given. There are many restrictions and high enforcement of the rules. If you were raised in an extremely controlling family, perhaps you experience great discomfort or anger whenever someone doesn't agree with you or behaves contrary to your ideas, advice, or rules.

Most people were raised in families in which the family atmosphere is somewhere between extremely warm and extremely hostile. Perhaps there was some hostility, but most of the time warmth was shown. Likewise, few people were raised on either extreme of independence or control. Most children are gradually granted more independence as they get older.

CONSIDERATIONS: You and your partner might find it difficult agreeing or cooperating on how to raise your children. You learned from different teachers! Now is the time for both of you to objectively appraise the benefits and drawbacks of your own upbringing, and purposely create the type of family atmosphere that is best for your family.

Your children need stability and consistency in their family life. When they are presented with dissimilar messages from you and your partner it may be quite difficult for them to develop a consistent value system. Although you both may not at present agree on certain techniques of child rearing, you must come to some agreement for the children's sake. Although compromise and cooperation may be difficult at first, you will find that the harmony they eventually produce will enhance your relationship and your family stability.

First, make compromises. Families function more smoothly when each partner practices the give-and-take process of cooperation. The will of one spouse should not impose on the rights of the other partner. Selfish desires of one partner may often lead to long-lasting hurts and resentments on the part of the other. Many compromises may not immediately feel good to the individual, but the cooperation and agreement lead to a more stable relationship.

Second, be consistent. When you agree upon how you will handle certain issues, tell the children about the process you went through to come to your decisions. That is, let them know that the rules of the house have been formulated by both you and your partner. When issues come up you may be tempted to go back to your old ways of dealing with them, but stay consistent for the family's sake. In the long run your children will respect the newfound strength of family unity.

Third, be patient. Change takes time. Your children will do their best to test the parent they see as the more lenient. At first expect a certain amount of protest when family rules are changed or added. But over time the children will realize that you and your spouse are together when it comes to discipline. Remember, a parent is a child's most influential teacher.

Your Name: _____*Samuel Larkings*_____ Date: ____*3-16-97*____

Partner's Name: ___*Sarah Rellings-Larkings*_____

PLEASE RESPOND TO THE FOLLOWING ITEMS. Do not share this information with your partner until the next counseling session.

1) Which of the following best describes the family in which you grew up?:

WARM AND ACCEPTING				AVERAGE				HOSTILE AND FIGHTING
1	2	3	4	5	6	7	⑧	9

COMMENTS: *My family was quite dysfunctional. What dad said was law, especially when he drank.*

2) Which of these describes the way in which your parents raised you?:

ALLOWED ME TO BE VERY INDEPENDENT				AVERAGE				ATTEMPTED TO CONTROL ME
1	②	3	4	5	6	7	8	9

COMMENTS: *My family had no consistent rules.*

3) Which of the following best describes the family in which your partner grew up?:

WARM AND ACCEPTING				AVERAGE				HOSTILE AND FIGHTING
①	2	3	4	5	6	7	8	9

COMMENTS: *Her family was very close, almost mushy.*

4) Which of these describes the way in which your partner's parents raised your partner?:

ALLOWED MY PARTNER TO BE VERY INDEPENDENT				AVERAGE				ATTEMPTED TO CONTROL MY PARTNER
1	2	3	④	5	6	7	8	9

COMMENTS: _____

5) Which of the following best describes YOUR family style?:

I AM WARM AND ACCEPTING				AVERAGE				I AM HOSTILE AND FIGHTING
1	2	3	4	5	6	⑦	8	9

COMMENTS: *I want my children to be able to handle themselves.*

_____

6) Which of these describes the way in which YOU are raising your children?:

```
I ALLOW THEM
  TO BE VERY                                                     I ATTEMPT TO
INDEPENDENT                        AVERAGE                       CONTROL THEM
     1        (2)      3       4       5       6       7       8       9
```

COMMENTS: *I want my children to learn to make their own decisions.*

7) Which of the following best describes YOUR PARTNER's family style?:

```
PARTNER IS                                                      PARTNER IS
WARM AND                                                        HOSTILE AND
ACCEPTING                          AVERAGE                      FIGHTING
   (1)        2       3       4       5       6       7       8       9
```

COMMENTS: *She lets the children get away with too much. When they are acting up she blames herself.*

8) Which of these describes the way in which YOUR PARTNER is raising your children?:

```
PARTNER ALLOWS                                                  PARTNER
THEM TO BE VERY                                                 ATTEMPTS TO
  INDEPENDENT                       AVERAGE                      CONTROL THEM
     1        2       3       4      (5)      6       7       8       9
```

COMMENTS: _____

9) Which of the following best describes the family style you would like YOU AND YOUR PARTNER to have?:

```
WARM AND                                                        HOSTILE AND
ACCEPTING                          AVERAGE                      FIGHTING
   1        2       3       4      (5)      6       7       8       9
```

COMMENTS: *A balance between the two extremes.*

10) Which of these describes the way in which you would like YOU AND YOUR PARTNER to raise your children?:

```
BOTH ALLOW                                                      BOTH
  TO BE VERY                                                    ATTEMPT TO
INDEPENDENT                        AVERAGE                      CONTROL THEM
     1        2       3       4      (5)      6       7       8       9
```

COMMENTS: _____

11) List the child-rearing issues about which you and your partner have very different opinions or practices:

A) ISSUE: _____ *Spanking* _____

    HOW DO YOU DIFFER?: *I spank the children when they don't obey. She believes in*
grounding or withholding rewards for punishment.

    PROBLEMS ARISING: *She gets very upset. I become the "bad guy." The*
children run to her when I get upset.

    YOUR WILLINGNESS TO COMPROMISE: *I will compromise if we can come up with*
a solution in which the children will mind us and respect our rules.

    COMMENTS: _____

B) ISSUE: *Bedtime for the children* _____

    HOW DO YOU DIFFER?: *Me: No set bedtimes, just be responsible.*
Her: A set time of 9:00 every night.

    PROBLEMS ARISING: *It causes confusion for the children. In this*
case, the children side with me and get upset at her.

    YOUR WILLINGNESS TO COMPROMISE: *Yes, if the children have some freedom*
in the matter.

    COMMENTS: _____

C) ISSUE: *Children's homework* _____

    HOW DO YOU DIFFER?: *Me: Do it when they want; if not, suffer the consequences.*
Her: Children must do homework before they can go outside and play.

    PROBLEMS ARISING: *Children don't like to do their homework.*

    YOUR WILLINGNESS TO COMPROMISE: *Same answer as #2 above.*

    COMMENTS: _____

D) ISSUE: *Allowances* _____

    HOW DO YOU DIFFER?: *Me: No allowances—children should earn money.*
Her: Set allowances, but basic chores should be completed most of the time.

    PROBLEMS ARISING: *We have different expectations of what the children*
should learn about the value of money. Children don't respect money.

    YOUR WILLINGNESS TO COMPROMISE: *I will try if we can come up*
with a solution.

    COMMENTS: _____

Cooperating in Child Rearing

No two people totally agree on all child-rearing principles. The same individual will often seem strict in some matters but quite lax in others. What you view as strict may be thought of as lenient by your partner. What you consider to be fun might be seen as dangerous by your partner.

Most parents tend to raise their children in a similar manner to how they grew up. Of course there are exceptions, but many of the child-rearing techniques we use were learned because our parents (by their example) taught them to us. Unless your parents were just like your partner's parents, your schooling was identical to your partner's schooling, your ideas are the same as your partner's ideas, and so forth, it is inevitable that some of your child-rearing techniques will conflict with those of your partner.

Two important issues involved in child-rearing practices include:

1) the degree of **warmth vs. hostility** in the household, and
2) the degree of **independence vs. control** rendered to the child.

1) WARMTH VS. HOSTILITY. The amount of warmth shown in a family can range from extremely warm (too much smothering and affection) to extremely hostile (little or no love shown).

Extremely warm families often smother their children with so much affection that the children may grow up demanding that others take care of their needs. If you were raised in an extremely warm family it is possible that you might have some difficulties separating your identity from that of your children and family.

Being raised in a warm, loving family can be quite rewarding provided that it doesn't lead to constant smothering. Warm families tend to be affectionate, accepting, and low in physical punishment; parents don't openly criticize one another and are family-centered, rather than self-centered.

Extremely hostile families are often prone to extreme disciplinary measures toward their children. The words "I love you" are rarely spoken. Parents are often rejecting, cold, disapproving, and quite critical of family members. If you were raised in a hostile family it is possible that you might have some difficulties listening to your children's points of view, showing affection, and controlling your temper.

Some families seem to go back and forth between warmth and hostility. When things are going quite well (e.g., children are obeying, finances are in order, parents are getting along, etc.) these families tend to be warm. But when pressures confront the family, there may be times when the parents vent their hostilities on each other and/or the children. This type of situation becomes confusing to the children because of the mixed messages they are receiving. These parents must learn how to be consistent.

2) INDEPENDENCE VS. CONTROL. The amount of independence granted to children can range from extreme independence (children having few or no rules) to extreme control (children allowed to make few or no decisions).

Extreme independence in a family allows the children to do almost whatever they want to do. Parents reason that the children will learn from their mistakes and grow from the experiences. Few restrictions are imposed, and little enforcement is provided for these restrictions. If you were raised in an extremely independent child-rearing family, it is quite possible that you are somewhat uncomfortable when it comes to setting limits or enforcing family rules.

Extreme control in a family allows few decisions to be made without the approval of the "head of the house." Children are expected to do exactly what they are told, even when no logical reason is given. There are many restrictions and high enforcement of the rules. If you were raised in an extremely controlling family, perhaps you experience great discomfort or anger whenever someone doesn't agree with you or behaves contrary to your ideas, advice, or rules.

Most people were raised in families in which the family atmosphere is somewhere between extremely warm and extremely hostile. Perhaps there was some hostility, but most of the time warmth was shown. Likewise, few people were raised on either extreme of independence or control. Most children are gradually granted more independence as they get older.

CONSIDERATIONS: You and your partner might find it difficult agreeing or cooperating on how to raise your children. You learned from different teachers! Now is the time for both of you to objectively appraise the benefits and drawbacks of your own upbringing, and purposely create the type of family atmosphere that is best for your family.

Your children need stability and consistency in their family life. When they are presented with dissimilar messages from you and your partner it may be quite difficult for them to develop a consistent value system. Although you both may not at present agree on certain techniques of child rearing, you must come to some agreement for the children's sake. Although compromise and cooperation may be difficult at first, you will find that the harmony they eventually produce will enhance your relationship and your family stability.

First, make compromises. Families function more smoothly when each partner practices the give-and-take process of cooperation. The will of one spouse should not impose on the rights of the other partner. Selfish desires of one partner may often lead to long-lasting hurts and resentments on the part of the other. Many compromises may not immediately feel good to the individual, but the cooperation and agreement lead to a more stable relationship.

Second, be consistent. When you agree upon how you will handle certain issues, tell the children about the process you went through to come to your decisions. That is, let them know that the rules of the house have been formulated by both you and your partner. When issues come up you may be tempted to go back to your old ways of dealing with them, but stay consistent for the family's sake. In the long run your children will respect the newfound strength of family unity.

Third, be patient. Change takes time. Your children will do their best to test the parent they see as the more lenient. At first expect a certain amount of protest when family rules are changed or added. But over time the children will realize that you and your spouse are together when it comes to discipline. Remember, a parent is a child's most influential teacher.

Your Name: _____ Date: _____
_____
Partner's Name: _____
PLEASE RESPOND TO THE FOLLOWING ITEMS. Do not share this information with your partner until the next counseling session.

1) Which of the following best describes the family in which you grew up?:

WARM AND   HOSTILE AND
ACCEPTING   AVERAGE   FIGHTING
    1   2   3   4   5   6   7   8   9

COMMENTS: _____

2) Which of these describes the way in which your parents raised you?:

ALLOWED ME
TO BE VERY   ATTEMPTED TO
INDEPENDENT   AVERAGE   CONTROL ME
    1   2   3   4   5   6   7   8   9

COMMENTS: _____

3) Which of the following best describes the family in which your partner grew up?:

WARM AND   HOSTILE AND
ACCEPTING   AVERAGE   FIGHTING
    1   2   3   4   5   6   7   8   9

COMMENTS: _____

4) Which of these describes the way in which your partner's parents raised your partner?:

ALLOWED MY
PARTNER   ATTEMPTED TO
TO BE VERY   CONTROL MY
INDEPENDENT   AVERAGE   PARTNER
    1   2   3   4   5   6   7   8   9

COMMENTS: _____

5) Which of the following best describes YOUR family style?:

I AM   I AM
WARM AND   HOSTILE AND
ACCEPTING   AVERAGE   FIGHTING
    1   2   3   4   5   6   7   8   9

COMMENTS: _____

6.37

6) Which of these describes the way in which YOU are raising your children?:

I ALLOW THEM
TO BE VERY
INDEPENDENT   AVERAGE   I ATTEMPT TO
CONTROL THEM

1   2   3   4   5   6   7   8   9

COMMENTS: _____

7) Which of the following best describes YOUR PARTNER's family style?:

PARTNER IS
WARM AND
ACCEPTING   AVERAGE   PARTNER IS
HOSTILE AND
FIGHTING

1   2   3   4   5   6   7   8   9

COMMENTS: _____

8) Which of these describes the way in which YOUR PARTNER is raising your children?:

PARTNER ALLOWS
THEM TO BE VERY
INDEPENDENT   AVERAGE   PARTNER
ATTEMPTS TO
CONTROL THEM

1   2   3   4   5   6   7   8   9

COMMENTS: _____

9) Which of the following best describes the family style you would like YOU AND YOUR PARTNER to have?:

WARM AND
ACCEPTING   AVERAGE   HOSTILE AND
FIGHTING

1   2   3   4   5   6   7   8   9

COMMENTS: _____

10) Which of these describes the way in which you would like YOU AND YOUR PARTNER to raise your children?:

BOTH ALLOW
TO BE VERY
INDEPENDENT   AVERAGE   BOTH
ATTEMPT TO
CONTROL THEM

1   2   3   4   5   6   7   8   9

COMMENTS: _____

11) List the child-rearing issues about which you and your partner have very different opinions or practices:

A) ISSUE: _____

HOW DO YOU DIFFER?: _____

_____

PROBLEMS ARISING: _____

_____

YOUR WILLINGNESS TO COMPROMISE: _____

_____

COMMENTS: _____

B) ISSUE: _____

HOW DO YOU DIFFER?: _____

_____

PROBLEMS ARISING: _____

_____

YOUR WILLINGNESS TO COMPROMISE: _____

_____

COMMENTS: _____

C) ISSUE: _____

HOW DO YOU DIFFER?: _____

_____

PROBLEMS ARISING: _____

_____

YOUR WILLINGNESS TO COMPROMISE: _____

_____

COMMENTS: _____

D) ISSUE: _____

HOW DO YOU DIFFER?: _____

_____

PROBLEMS ARISING: _____

_____

YOUR WILLINGNESS TO COMPROMISE: _____

_____

COMMENTS: _____

Sharing
Your Feelings

In the form on pages 6.41 and 6.42 couples are asked to complete sentences in the presence of their partner in which opportunities are given to discuss their commitment to the relationship. This exercise has been helpful for individuals who have difficulties expressing their feelings.

Sharing Your Feelings

Your Name: _____Sergio Allecio_____ Date: __4-2-97__
Spouse's Name: _____Monica Allecio_____

DIRECTIONS: Both partners are to face each other, hold hands, and look into one another's eyes during the following communication assignment.

Both partners take turns reading and elaborating on each of the following statements. One partner is first to share feelings on the odd-numbered items, while the other partner is first on the even-numbered items. Both partners respond to all items.

Do not make any remarks regarding your partner's statements. Just listen attentively.

Do not write down your spouse's responses during the exercise. When you have completed all the items write down what you remember from your partner's responses.

1) I fell in love with you because ___you treated me better than anyone else had ever treated me. You were special to me.___

2) You make me so happy when you _tell me that you love me._

3) I'm sorry about __blaming you every time we have money problems.__

4) I wish we could _talk about things before we blow up at each other._

5) To help you be more happy I should probably _let you know that I believe in you._

6) We need to spend more time __making future plans and sticking to them.__

7) I am lonely when __we argue and don't talk for a while.__

8) I am proud of you when __you play so well with the children even though I know you are very busy.__

9) You seem to get angry when I _act as if your opinion is not important to me._

10) Try to understand that I ___think the world of you.___

11) I'll try to stop _acting like only my opinion counts._

12) One thing I need more of from you is _thanks for all I do around the house that rarely is appreciated._

13) It is hard for me to express my feelings about _how upset I get when you seem to be flirting with other women._

14) To make our relationship better I will _look at marriage as a partnership and treat you the way I want to be treated._

15) We need to stop _competing and being one up on the other._

16) We need to start _acting like we are married and love each other._

17) If we try, I believe we can _renew our commitment—this time for good._

18) We seem to stop communicating whenever _it seems like one of us is right and the other is not._

19) We need better planning when it comes to _finances and spending._

20) The one thing that has changed the most in our relationship is _how we treat each other. The level of respect has really gotten poor._

21) It is getting harder for me to _confide in you, because when we argue you use it against me._

22) A happy marriage (or relationship) means that _each person puts the relationship first, but is allowed to be an individual._

23) Whatever it takes, I will _make compromises to make this marriage grow._

24) I wish we could somehow go back to the time when _we wouldn't even think of cutting down the other person._

25) We don't understand each other when it comes to _the give-and-take process in a happy marriage._

26) I don't understand how to please you when _you ask my opinion about something, but almost never follow my advice. It's like you want to do the opposite._

27) I feel guilty after _I throw your mistakes in your face._

28) I get scared whenever _you seem to care more about the women at work than me._

29) Please help me to _be myself._

Sharing Your Feelings

Your Name: _____ Date: _____

Spouse's Name: _____

DIRECTIONS: Both partners are to face each other, hold hands, and look into one another's eyes during the following communication assignment.

Both partners take turns reading and elaborating on each of the following statements. One partner is first to share feelings on the odd-numbered items, while the other partner is first on the even-numbered items. Both partners respond to all items.

Do not make any remarks regarding your partner's statements. Just listen attentively.

Do not write down your spouse's responses during the exercise. When you have completed all the items write down what you remember from your partner's responses.

1) I fell in love with you because _____
_____

2) You make me so happy when you _____
_____

3) I'm sorry about _____
_____

4) I wish we could _____
_____

5) To help you be more happy I should probably _____
_____

6) We need to spend more time _____
_____

7) I am lonely when _____
_____

8) I am proud of you when _____
_____

9) You seem to get angry when I _____
_____

10) Try to understand that I _____
_____

11) I'll try to stop _____
   _____

12) One thing I need more of from you is _____
   _____

13) It is hard for me to express my feelings about _____
   _____

14) To make our relationship better I will _____
   _____

15) We need to stop _____
   _____

16) We need to start _____
   _____

17) If we try, I believe we can _____
   _____

18) We seem to stop communicating whenever _____
   _____

19) We need better planning when it comes to _____
   _____

20) The one thing that has changed the most in our relationship is _____
   _____

21) It is getting harder for me to _____
   _____

22) A happy marriage (or relationship) means that _____
   _____

23) Whatever it takes, I will _____
   _____

24) I wish we could somehow go back to the time when _____
   _____

25) We don't understand each other when it comes to _____
   _____

26) I don't understand how to please you when _____
   _____

27) I feel guilty after _____
   _____

28) I get scared whenever _____
   _____

29) Please help me to _____
   _____

Bibliography and Suggested Readings

American Psychiatric Association. (1994). *Diagnostic and Statistic Manual of Mental Disorders* (4th ed.). Washington, DC: American Psychiatric Association.

American Psychological Association. (1992). *Ethical Principles for Psychologists and Code of Conduct.* Washington, DC: American Psychological Association.

———. (1987). General Guidelines for Providers of Psychological Services. *American Psychologist, 42,* 7.

Barlow, D. H. (1993). *Clinical Handbook of Psychological Disorders: A Step-by-Step Treatment Manual* (2d ed.). New York, NY: Guilford Press.

Brown, S. L. (1991). *The Quality Management Professional's Study Guide.* Pasadena, CA: Managed Care Consultants.

Browning, C. H. (1996). "Practice Survival Strategies: Business Basics for Effective Marketing to Managed Care." In N. A. Cummings, et al. (Eds.), *Surviving the Demise of Solo Practice: Mental Health Practitioners Prospering in the Era of Managed Care.* New York, NY: Psychosocial Press.

Browning, C. H., & Browning, B. J. (1996). *How to Partner with Managed Care.* New York, NY: John Wiley & Sons, Inc.

Galasso, D. (1987). "Guidelines for Developing Multi-Disciplinary Treatment Plans." *Hospital and Community Psychiatry, 38,* 394–397.

Goldstein, G., & Hersen, M. (1990). *Handbook of Psychological Assessment* (2d ed.). New York, NY: Pergamon Press.

Goodman, M., Brown, J., & Deitz, P. (1992). *Managing Managed Care: A Mental Health Practitioner's Guide.* Washington, DC: American Psychiatric Press.

Grant, R. L. (1981). "The Capacity of the Psychiatric Record to Meet Changing Needs." In C. Siegel & S. K. Fischer (Eds.), *Psychiatric Records in Mental Health Care.* New York, NY: Brunner/Mazel.

Groth-Marnat, G. (1990). *Handbook of Psychological Assessment* (2d ed.). New York, NY: John Wiley & Sons, Inc.

Joint Commission on Accreditation of Healthcare Organizations. (1994). *Accreditation Manual for Mental Health, Chemical Dependency, and Mental Retardation Developmental Disabilities Services.* OakBrook Terrace, IL: Joint Commission on Accreditation of Healthcare Organizations.

Jongsma, A. E., & Peterson, L. M. (1995). *The Complete Psychotherapy Treatment Planner.* New York, NY: John Wiley & Sons, Inc.

Jongsma, A. E., Peterson, L. M., & McInnis, W. P. (1996). *The Child and Adolescent Psychotherapy Treatment Planner*. New York, NY: John Wiley & Sons, Inc.

Kennedy, J. A. (1992). *Fundamentals of Psychiatric Treatment Planning*. Washington, DC: American Psychiatric Press.

Maxmen, J. S., & Ward, N. G. (1995). *Essential Psychopathology and Its Treatment*. New York, NY: W. W. Norton, Inc.

*Medicare Program: Prospective Payment for Medicare Final Rule. Federal Register 49 (January 3):*234–240. (1984).

Morrison, J. R. (1993). *The First Interview*. New York, NY: Guilford Press.

Othmer, E., & Othmer, S. C. (1994). *The Clinical Interview Using DSM IV*, Vol. 1: *Fundamentals;* Vol. 2: *The Difficult Patient*. Washington, DC: American Psychiatric Press.

Phares, E. J. (1988). *Clinical Psychology: Concepts, Methods, and Profession* (3d ed.). Pacific Grove, CA: Brooks/Cole Publishing Co.

Social Security Regulations. (1981). *Rules for Determining Disability and Blindness*. Washington, DC: U.S. Department of Health and Human Services, Social Security Administration, Office of Operational Policy and Procedures, SSA No. 64-014, ICN 436850.

Soreff, S. M., & McDuffee, M. A. (1993). *Documentation Survival Handbook: A Clinician's Guide to Charting for Better Care, Certification, Reimbursement, and Risk Management*. Seattle, WA: Hogrefe & Huber.

Trzepacz, P. T., & Baker, R. W. (1993). *The Psychiatric Mental Status Examination*. New York, NY: Oxford University Press.

U.S. Department of Health and Human Services. (1983). Medicare Program: Prospective Payments for Medicare Inpatient Hospital Services. *Federal Register 48(171):*39752-890.

Zuckerman, E. L. (1995). *Clinician's Thesaurus: A Guidebook for Writing Psychological Reports*. New York, NY: Guilford Press.

Zuckerman, E. L. & Guyett, I. P. R. (in press). *The Paper Office* (4th ed.). New York, NY: Guilford Press.

Disk Information

Disk Table of Contents

Introduction

The enclosed disk contains 24 forms saved in Microsoft Word version 2.0 format. In order to use the files you need to have Microsoft Word version 2.0 or higher, or other word processing software capable of reading Microsoft Word 2.0 files.

After installing the files to your hard drive (see instructions below), you can open the files in your word processor and print the forms or begin customizing them to suit your needs. You may want to add or delete text, adjust the formatting, reset margins and tabs, change fonts, etc. Refer to the user manual that came with your word processing software for instructions on how to make these changes.

System Requirements

- IBM PC or compatible computer

- 3.5″ floppy disk drive

- Windows 3.1 or higher

- Microsoft Word version 2.0 or higher, or other word processing software (such as WordPerfect for Windows) capable of reading Microsoft Word 2.0 files.

How to Install the Files onto Your Computer

The enclosed disk contains files saved in Microsoft Word version 2.0. Running the installation program will copy the files to your hard drive in the default directory C:\WIGER. To run the installation program, do the following:

1. Insert the enclosed disk into the floppy disk drive of your computer.

2. Windows 3.1: From the Program Manager, choose File, Run.

   Windows 95: From the Start Menus, choose Run.

3. Type **A:\INSTALL** and press Enter.

4. The opening screen of the installation program will appear. Press Enter to continue.

5. The default destination directory is C:\WIGER. If you wish to change the default destination, you may do so now. Follow the instructions on the screen.

6. The installation program will copy all files to your hard drive in the C:\WIGER or user-designated directory.

Using the Files

In order to use the files you need to load your word processing program. Instructions on opening the files with Microsoft Word and WordPerfect are provided below.

   Note: Many popular word processing programs (including WordPerfect for Windows) are capable of reading Microsoft Word files. However, users should be aware that a slight amount of formatting may be lost when using a program other than Microsoft Word. Also, some users may need to readjust tabs and page margins because of the default font type and default margins set in their program.

USING THE FILES WITH MICROSOFT WORD FOR WINDOWS

To use the files with Microsoft Word for Windows, do the following:

1. Load the Microsoft Word for Windows program.

2. When the blank document screen is displayed, select Open from the File menu.

3. The Open dialog box will appear. Make the appropriate selections for the drive and directory. If you installed to the default directory the files will be located in the **C:\WIGER** directory.

4. In the file name list, double click on the file you want to open.

   You can make any changes or revisions to the document.

5. To print the file, select PRINT from the FILE menu.

USING THE FILES WITH WORDPERFECT FOR WINDOWS

To use the files with WordPerfect for Windows, do the following:

1. Load the WordPerfect for Windows program.

2. When the blank document screen is displayed, select Open from the File Menu.

3. The Open dialog box will appear. Make the appropriate selections for the drive and directory. If you installed to the default directory the files will be located in the **C:\WIGER** directory.

4. To see a list of all files, under Type of Files select ALL FILES (*.*).

5. In the file name list, double click on the file you want to open.

6. The file will immediately load into WordPerfect for Windows.

   You can make any changes or revisions to the document.

7. To print the file, select PRINT from the FILE menu.

SAVING FILES

When you have finished editing a document, you should save it under a new file name before exiting your word processing program.

User Assistance

If you need basic assistance with installation or if you have a damaged disk, please call our product support number at (212) 850-6194 weekdays between 9 A.M. and 4 P.M. Eastern Standard Time.

To place additional orders or to request information about other Wiley products, please call (800) 225-5945.